Friend in Your Pocket ;>)!!!!

Your "Spirit Personal Trainer"

When Social Networking isn't enough; an additional resource for helping you make the only connection that truly matters... The connection to Your "Self"!

Fits in All Gym Bags

Fits in All Purses

Qwana M. "BabyGirl" Reynolds-Frasier

1-GPS (God Positioning System)

Friend In Your Pocket

For All Inquires Contact:

FriendInYourPocket.Com
FriendInYourPocket@Aol.Com

Friend In Your Pocket Inc. Publisher

2-GPS (God Positioning System)

Friend In Your Pocket

International Standard Book Number

978-0-9892769-1-7

Library of Congress Catalog No.

18-06468

3-GPS (God Positioning System)

07/27/13 To Michee Poo! :>)♡

Friend In Your Pocket AKA

Thanks for Supporting Michele

So Glad Your Have Started This
Journey ;>)!!!!

God Bless You

Stay Positive God Has
you!♡

Love Always♡

4-GPS (God Positioning System)

Friend In Your Pocket

Table of Contents

5-GPS (God Positioning System)

Friend In Your Pocket

6-GPS (God Positioning System)

Friend In Your Pocket

7-GPS (God Positioning System)

Friend In Your Pocket

8-GPS (God Positioning System)

Friend In Your Pocket

9-GPS (God Positioning System)

Friend In Your Pocket

10-GPS (God Positioning System)

Friend In Your Pocket

11-GPS (God Positioning System)

Friend In Your Pocket

12-GPS (God Positioning System)

Friend In Your Pocket

13-GPS (God Positioning System)

Friend In Your Pocket

14-GPS (God Positioning System)

__My Page of Gratitude...__

My, "Ride or Die", My "Best Buddy", My Loyal Companion "Who Was With Me Shooting in The Gym" Big Dre You're the Very Best Partner A Woman Can Ask For. Thanks Buddy, "Teamwork, Work Hard" ;>)!!!! We Gon' Give The World This Work ;>)!!!!

My Sons DeDe and Moose.

DeDe You are my second lesson in selfless love. Although you drive me crazy you have made me a better person because you were born. You are on the Brink of Your Breakthrough. Thank You for Choosing Me Muahhhh ;>)!!!!

15-GPS (God Positioning System)

Friend In Your Pocket

Moose my third lesson; My Rock
with the Mushy Interior, You
Rock!!!! You have the biggest heart
and you are the kindest generous
soul. Keep striving you are
"Destined" for Greatness. Your
Breakthrough is in Your Hands,
Shoot the Ball. Let's Get It ;>)!!!!

Dwayne you are my oldest brother,
my first protector, Thank you for
showing me how a woman should be
treated. You taught me that showing
emotions are for everybody not just
girls. You are a wonderful father. I
love you ;>)!!!!

My Brother My Twin Anthony; we
have been tight since day one and
nothing has changed. We argue, we
debate, we brainstorm, we build and
now we have the foundation for our

16-GPS (God Positioning System)

Empire. Thanks for keeping me on my toes and being humble enough to wave the pompoms as you cheer for me unconditionally. Thank You ;>)!!!!

To My Big Sis Raci you have always pushed me, motivated me, and inspired me to be a fierce woman. Thank you for trusting me with your inner thoughts and feelings. Love you Muahhhh ;>)!!!!

To My Favorite Redhead Rashaad, I love you. We fight, we argue, we make up, and we go to Miami ;>)!!!! We have grown all the way up together and I am very proud of the Man you are. I just push you hard because I know that you're a warrior and you will always rise to the occasion. Thank you for being my first lesson in selfless love ;>)!!!!

To Mommy, You are my blueprint thanks for letting me in. You're honest, loyal, and believed the vision since day one. You are my spiritual compass and you have taught me so much. Thank you for showing me that "Another Chance" is possible if you want it bad enough. You are Simply the Best Muahhhh ;>)!!!!

To My Pops, Thank you for showing me the raw uncut that has given me my depth. You and Mom made me a dynamic spirit. You named me, "Qwana" an African flower that sits by the River. In this river of life I have enduring strength as I sway back and forth with the tides of life.

18-GPS (God Positioning System)

Friend In Your Pocket

Thanks for the constant reminder it is
a "Blessing" ;>)!!!!

19-GPS (God Positioning System)

Words=Sword

Let this Sword cut through the pain
of the day before to reveal a new
skin and a new "Us"; free of the dead
skin of the lifetime before!

~Me

This Book is dedicated to the Frasier
and Reynolds Families for Your
Blankets of Love, Support and
Belief. You Are All I Need In This
Life of Sinless Bliss ;>)!!!!

Also I Will Always Remember The
First Person To Indoctrinate Me and
Introduce Me To The Wonderful
Whimsical World of Literature, Ned
O'Gorman Thank You ;>)!!!! I am
Eternally Grateful <3

Friend In Your Pocket

To my Storm Chaser; "The Justice Wrangler", my attorney at law Justine Olderman. You came at a desperate time and helped to turn It into the Sweetest Revenge Slice of Humble Pie. God Brought Me The Woman of Justice When My Sanity and Faith Was Tested.

A Trillion Thanks and an Infinite Well of the Waters of Gratitude Flow for All of Those Who Have Encouraged Me A long "Our" Journey. I Love You With All My Being.

To My Survivors of Anything Lets Show This World What We Can Do When We Take The Cloud Of Trauma Off and Replace It With Success and the Deed of Paying It Forward.

21-GPS (God Positioning System)

Glory Be to God!!!!

Indoctrination to The Reintroduction of Old Fashion Values

In a world obsessed with Social Networking, Facebooking, Blogging, Texting, Emailing, BBMing, Vining, Twittering, Instagraming, Skyping, Oovooing, Pin Interesting, Snap Chatting, Tumblring, KiKing etc. We have lost the "Human Connection", Friendship, Brotherhood, Sisterhood; the personal touch of a relationship and sense of family are being devalued in our defiant society.

In a world at War, Recession, Depression, Racism, Hyper-Sexualization, Violence, Drug Abuse, Jealousy, Low Self Esteem,

Friend In Your Pocket

Lack of Emphasis on Education,
Compassion, and Empathy we face
strenuous challenges due in part to
wide spread Selfishness; which
blocks "Real" communication
between person to person.

In this struggle between our virtual
world and our reality worlds we have
lost sight of the fact that a single
word of encouragement from another
human being has the ability to
change a person's "Life". A brief
earnest, sincere interaction can uplift,
inspire, and motivate someone to
change or to change his or her mind.

This book was birthed with "Us" in
mind.

My family and friends have always
expressed how much they appreciate

24-GPS (God Positioning System)

my insight, spirit-filled outlook and quotes. The irony is that I would realize the need for a book such as this one through the "Gift" of Social Networking (I am in favor of Social Networking in Moderation) ;>)!!!! Social Networking should not replace an In Person Visit, Telephone Call, a Birthday Card, a Thank You Card, a Girl's Night Out, A Guy's Night on the Town, an Invitation etc. The collective yearning for deep personal connections was evident through the outpouring of Comments, Likes, Re-Post, and Inbox Messages I would receive daily.

It was clear that our connection through, "Friend in Your Pocket" was necessary however our

25-GPS (God Positioning System)

"lifestyles" do not always foster the time thought to be needed to make these connections. We are constantly on the go, multi-tasking between family, career, relationships, bills, dreams, reality, etc. We find ourselves with not enough minutes in the hour, not enough hours in the day, and not enough months in the year :>(!!!!

Have you ever noticed almost everyone you speak to has the tendency to tell you that they are, "Soooo Tired" (The Terrible "T" word) and we all know that the "T" word is contagious, right???? LOL ;>)!!!! As soon as someone says, the Terrible "T" word to you and suddenly you feel a little sluggish and get an urge to yawn ;>). Moving forward let us stop claiming the tired spirit and let us tell the truth: we may be sleepy, or just downright confused with our current state of being.

People on their deathbeds often say that they are tired signaling to end of their life journey. Are you nearing your life's journey that you know of???? If not stop saying you are tired.

This is why it is so important that when we are afforded a "moment" to ourselves; where our minds are clear, open, and thirsty for inspiration, we must get what we need and we must get it in hurry!!!!

Here is Inspiration for the Friend on the Go ;>)!!!!

27-GPS (God Positioning System)

Friend In Your Pocket

Welcome to the beginning of our "Grass Roots Movement", where Inspiration is the "Blue Plate Special" in our Diner being served however you like it daily, 365 days a year and 24 hours a day. Together we will grow One Day, One Friend, One Family, and One Nation at a time. By now I know that you are beginning to realize why, "Friend in Your Pocket" is such an important literary work (Well at least I Hope you do ;>)

When the "National Grid" and other power sources are down or when the connection to your server has been lost, "Friend in Your Pocket" will always be here to encourage you to follow your dreams, believe in hope, love, and be loved the Agape way

28-GPS (God Positioning System)

(Unconditionally), accept and cope with loss, embrace our differences, grow, and most importantly forgive your persecutors or forgive yourself (Sometimes we are our own worst persecutor).

There is a saying I love... "He, who walks with the wise, grows wise".

So in this spirit I say; "Those who bathe in Hope smell like it"

Thank you for bathing in Hope today, may we all continue to add our own unique sweet fragrance of growth, positivity, inspiration, and creativity to our world ;>)!!!!

"Friend in Your Pocket" is an everyday reader that will provide all of us with sustainable joy, spiritual focus, inspiration, motivation, and

29-GPS (God Positioning System)

hope. I encourage you "My Friend" to read this book in any order you wish at anytime; you are guaranteed to be thought provoked and challenged to rationalize from a different prospective.

When a friend in the "Human" form is emotionally, mentally, and physically unavailable to you "Friend in Your Pocket" can be your rock to lean on and a source to draw inspiration from; it is my hope that we will no longer feel empty. This book is going to fill you up and sustain your spiritual void.

I am not just a "Friend in Your Pocket" now I am a Friend in your Heart and Spirit... Or as Wendy Williams always says... "A Friend in Your Head" ;>)!!!!

30-GPS (God Positioning System)

Friend In Your Pocket

Blessings and Love to All Muahhhh
<3

Your Friend,

Qwana "BabyGirl" Reynolds Frasier

31-GPS (God Positioning System)

<u>Rise and Shine Sunshine ;>)!!!!</u>

Today is the beginning of another day we are all blessed to see, smell, enjoy, and live!!!! Yay ;>)!!!!

Are you ready for your Breakthrough ;>)????

Yes You Are... Let's Get It!!!!

Let us start to begin each day with a prayer; make sure your prayer is intentional and thoughtful. Make sure whatever you are praying for each day is what you truly desire.

A wonderful prayer for those of us embarking on a "Breakthrough Journey" is, "The Jabez Prayer" from the Holy Bible Kings James Version 1 Chronicles 4:10.

Friend In Your Pocket

"Jabez cried out to the God of Israel, "Oh, that you would bless me and enlarge my territory! Let your hand be with me, and keep me from harm so that I will be free from pain"

And God granted his request.

This is a short-winded powerful prayer filled with intentional thoughts.

I have said this prayer and it works, however you must be obedient and prepare yourself to put in the work needed to make this request come to fruition.

Once you begin to walk in your purpose the Lord will increase your terrain so you better invest in some good hiking shoes; this can be a

33-GPS (God Positioning System)

never-ending journey, if you so desire to climb higher ;>).

Most mornings one of two things happen either we are jarred out of sleep by our alarm clock in the external form or we are awakened by our internal alarm clocks. Our internal alarm clocks often sound off earlier than the external ones that wake us up so that we are not awakened by the external annoying counterpart ;>) LOL With Myself included some of us get up before the alarm goes off because we dislike hearing that beep beep beep. Do you know what this means? This means we are not even sleeping peacefully, what a shame ;>(!!!! We are thinking about alarm clocks while we sleep.

Friend In Your Pocket

Once we jump out of our beds and make them up (or not ;>) we usually keep going until it is time to get back into our beds later on that evening.

This is what I call, "The Hamster Wheel Cycle and this continues for most of our lives unless we do something about it.

And we thought our childhood pet hamster running around in circles was a sad sight LOL ;>)!!!! Now look at us...

Let us challenge ourselves to no longer: jump, leap, drag, or roll out of our beds. When we rise lets lay there, meditate, pray with intention, take deep intentional breathes, and listen to our hearts while we think of

"What" makes us grateful to be a part of this new day.

Once we have done so, let us affirm to ourselves that we are going to have a day filled with "Joy"; no matter what may take place throughout our day we will always find a moment of gratitude and see the positive in every suspected negative situation. I use the word "suspected" because positivity can reside in negativity if you are open to the idea of possessing an "Attitude of Gratitude". Are you open to this?

My brothers would often laugh at me when I would tell them, "I go to sleep "Joyful" I wake up "Joy-filled", but the problem is what happens in the middle of my day. The middle of the day is where most of our issues come from, right???? For my brothers it was no wonder why they found it funny because they often find themselves a part of that "Proverbial Middle" ;>).

So to this notion we have to say to ourselves, "No one will control my middle!!!!" The middle is our core from which we draw our strength physically, mentally, and spiritually. If our core is weak and filled with bleakness, anger, aggravation, and confusion, it will dictate the way we go to sleep and how we feel when we rise. Hence the cycle continues until we remove the junk out of your core, with the help of our "Mental Personal Trainer" "Friend in your Pocket" we will get our cores into tip top shape in no time ;>)!!!!

37-GPS (God Positioning System)

Friend In Your Pocket

*"I don't think of myself as a poor
deprived ghetto girl who made good.
I think of myself as somebody who
from an early age knew I was
responsible for myself, and I had to
make good".*

Thank You Ms. Oprah Winfrey;>)!!!!

*I have accepted my Divine "Call to
Duty", Humbly and Intentionally.*

**Inspiration is the light that escapes
through the darkness.**

**Let "Us" be afraid of the dark no
longer.**

38-GPS (God Positioning System)

Got Hustle ;>)????

This word Hustle is usually considered a negative act, however it is so very positive. Hustle is a verb, it is movement, and it is action. We all must possess equal parts of hustle, humility, determination, dedication, and hope to make our dreams comes true.

A Hustler is able to get multiple tasks done at a moment's notice with accuracy. A Hustler is knowledgeable about many things and realizes that this supersedes having mastery in only one particular area. Most awesome parents, employers, employees, friends, etc. are considered the, "Jacks of All Trades".

39-GPS (God Positioning System)

Friend In Your Pocket

Never get overly specialized in just one discipline, learn many.

Opportunity knocks and calls at any time of the day or night; so be well prepared when your number is called.

When one niche does not work out move on to the next; the important thing is that you never stop experimenting, growing, learning, and most of all moving.

Conjure the spirit of a Hustler everyday ;>)!!!! Heck Jesus was the, "Quintessential Hustler" he was a carpenter, a teacher, a visionary, a trusted confidant, and so much more. Jesus is the creator of this premise; how could the Hustle be wrong ;>)????

40-GPS (God Positioning System)

Friend In Your Pocket

You Can't Knock the Hustle!!!!

Thanks Jay-Z for making this word
Hustler a positive adjective ;>)

41-GPS (God Positioning System)

<u>You Are A Savior ;>)!!!!</u>

You are a **H.E.R.O**!!!!

Did you know that?

You are the…

Hope

Everyone

Relies

On

Friend In Your Pocket

People are waiting for you to shift their atmosphere with your talents and make a positive impact on their lives.

So go out and save someone today but remember to start with yourself "First" ;>)!!!!

God Speed!!!!

This thought was inspired by Mariah Carey's song, "Hero".

Thanks Emancipated Mimi, You are one of my SHEROS ;>)!!!!

Friend In Your Pocket

<u>You Future Has Legs Too!!!!</u>

Are you in a state of constant F.E.A.R? Do you believe you will not succeed?

Do you feel like someone already stole your breakthrough idea or moment?

Remember "Nobody" can do it like you can, revise the idea and add your personal flare to it.

If you continue to live in F.E.A.R you will witness your…

Future

Escaping

And

Running away from you.

44-GPS (God Positioning System)

Friend In Your Pocket

Lay your fears down throw caution to the wind. Tell the world, "I am coming through!!!!"

They have never seen a storm such as yours and never will if you don't overcome your fears of success.

Only Fear God; if you are living your life in accordance to the word of God, whom shall you fear but God.

Obedience is Key, Fear Not!!!!

God is like a great retirement fund that will match your efforts dollar for dollar ;>) There is no way you can lose.

Now in the words of Legendary Comedian Martin Lawrence…

"Get to Stepping" ;>) LOL!!!!

45-GPS (God Positioning System)

You Own Experience But You Can Borrow It From Others As Well;>)

Experience is a teacher, healer, memory, a guide of what to do or what not to do in the future etc. Most importantly your life experience is "Yours"!

Owning an experience is like owing your own property. When you own something or possess anything that thing gives you a great sense of pride, you take great care of it; you build it up, you fix whatever is broken, and when you have the finished product you show it off with pride.

While "Going Through" negative experiences keep in mind that one-day it "Will Be" a teachable moment.

46-GPS (God Positioning System)

Friend In Your Pocket

The house of experience is your own and yours alone, take care of it and share it, open your home to others in need of your expertise brought to you courtesy of experience.

If experience is a great teacher what is inexperience? Remember you do not have to go through negative experiences to be well rounded. Pay attention to the world around you these experiences, are happening all around you near and far. Let the experiences of others be your teacher. Be open and empathetic to the plight of others so that you may be able to help yourself.

Why Re-Invent the broken wheel ;>/????

<u>Have You Lost Something :>)????</u>

When you lose something you are always instructed to backtrack your last steps. What do you do when you lose yourself? If you subscribe to the notion of back tracking your steps, you must go back to your beginnings. You are sure to find yourself as well as the reason you were lost in the first place in a hiding place known as, "Childhood Traumas".

You can overcome!!!!

<u>Acute Inspiration Can Lead to Chronic Disease</u>

"Inspiration comes acutely however the results of being inspired are chronic"

When we have a spark of inspiration it can happen all of a sudden or it can come out of nowhere in the unlikeliest of places. Inspirational; moment may happen: during a situation, a word, a song, a story, a touch, a feeling, this book even, etc.; that inspires you. Understand that although it might have happened all of a sudden; the after effects will last and linger in your memory and spirit forever. Guess what...This is no coincidence.

49-GPS (God Positioning System)

Friend In Your Pocket

Never miss an opportunity to let inspiration take hold of you. Let me share a quick story if I may :>)!!!! I took a class a long time ago and it was family development based course on how to effectively work with impoverished youth and their families. One of our assignments was to look at a picture of a mother and child in a junky room and from this picture we had to list all the positive attributes in the picture.

Although this was a junky room we were able to identify that the mother had an iron, she ironed clothes, she had food, she was attempting to clean, she had a television, the child had toys, the child appeared comfortable, and most importantly the family had a safe place to call home.

This was not only inspiring but it was enlightening, it taught me a valuable lesson about what we are trained to see rather than what we should be seeing. I learned to look deeper before I looked at the surface. I was taught to see what was strong instead of what was wrong and to stray away from speaking to the deficits. I learned to, "Speak Life". I learned from a piece of paper and was grateful for it.

This lesson resonates in my soul on a daily basis. Thank You Lesson One Million and... LOL ;>)!!!!

Friend In Your Pocket

This is just one example of acute inspiration with chronic life altering effects.

Let's stay inspired and hopeful. Inspiration should be all of our "Chronic Wellness" disease ;>)!!!!

52-GPS (God Positioning System)

Curtain Call

Life is my "Muse" and Experience is my focal point that leads me to my visualizations and the source of my future.

Visualizations are different than living a life of grandeur; it is living your life to its fullest potential. Most of us have been told that we are not better or greater than our current living conditions. A lot of us have been told that we are crazy to visualize and execute our life goals. Being told, you are not better than or being called crazy to dare to dream is simply a pile of rubbish.

Live your life as though you have accomplished your dreams; this is your dress rehearsal and one should

practice every day until your dream
is reality.

When the curtain opens on this
Broadway Stage called Life you will
know every line and own your
leading role.

Stay Prepared :>)!!!!

Friend In Your Pocket

It Will Change You For Better Or For ...

If you say something enough times you can "Will It" to be your destiny... Your thoughts provoke actions thus producing shifts; this can be a positive thought as well as a negative thought. Be careful what you speak and who you speak into your life. Make every word and desire have intentions that are clear. You will begin to see changes within yourself immediately.

Get Ready, Set, Go ;>)!!!!

God is Awesome and Yes He is a Mind Reader, so watch your thoughts.

He can hear those too LOL ;>).

55-GPS (God Positioning System)

Friend In Your Pocket

Be The Store That Never Closes

The state of being, "Open" is not anything to be ashamed of; actually it is a gift from the Almighty God. Say it loud and say it proud. You have come into your true self. You are now open to receive and give love openly. To be open is a vulnerable state when your weak and broken in spirit however when you are knowledgeable, rooted, secure in yourself, and your beliefs being open is the ability to be ready for anything that comes your way; including wealth, love, and all the possibilities God has to offer. To be "Closed" is a sure fire way to miss an opportunity.

Stay Open like 7-11, never miss a sale, and you will be spiritually wealthy for the rest of your days ;>).

56-GPS (God Positioning System)

<u>The Office Is A Great Launch Location :>)</u>

I love the work place it gives us an outlet to meet people that we probably would have never known if all of us had not found ourselves in our current careers. Some of our co workers are funny, annoying, story tellers, spiritual, stinky, great cooks, love to celebrate holidays, some lie (and we all know it), some are always happy, some always complain, etc.

Most importantly over time they become a part of our families, our work family ;>).

I have seen a trend where some people have outgrown their careers but are scared and fearful to leave because they will leave the nest, so to speak. They will lose their work family, and that is understandable. Please remember that your work family is only a visit or phone call away.

When we have outgrown our current careers ask the Lord to, "Enlarge Your Territory" (The Jabez Prayer) He will... Please believe your work family will always be there for you, but you must leave the nest if you have an urge to. Your flight to, "Destiny Island" is on the tarmac waiting to take off. Don't let this flight leave without you ;>).

There is a phenomenon that happens once someone at work is courageous enough to make the change. I have you ever notice that funny thing that happens :>)???? Once one person leaves a particular work place, it becomes a domino effect and it usually starts a chain reaction of people pretending to be working while filling out job applications or faxing and emailing resumes all around town. Does that sound familiar???? LOL

That is why it is important for you to; "Be The Change You Want to See" (Thanks Gandhi) Your actions may spark the hidden potential in those around you while setting a flame to your own behind; a two-fer one is always a win, win ;>).

Never be afraid to leave your comfort zone. Be afraid to stay at the party past your curfew.

Friend In Your Pocket

Get Out While Your Spirit is Still
Alive ;>)!!!!

60-GPS (God Positioning System)

<u>Energy Is A Stock We All Own;>)!!!!</u>

We often talk about the importance of spending our money wisely however we do not extend that same courtesy to our energy. Without energy we cannot go out and make the money; so which one should be your top priority?

For the rest of our days moving forward let us say:

I will be expending my energy wisely!!!!

Energy=Vitality

So if something does not give you positive energy in exchange for the positive energy you put into it walk away; it is the beginning to look a lot

61-GPS (God Positioning System)

Friend In Your Pocket

like a bad investment that will not
yield any positive growth this quarter
and beyond.

Got Fizz ;>)????

Here is an experiment that most of us have conducted either intentionally or by mistake...

Shake a bottle of soda, watch the bubbles get agitated with nowhere to go, then open it and watch the agitated beverage spill and spurt all over the place (What a mess). Now close it and when you open it again, what happens? The soda is flat and has lost its fizz.

All of its energy was expended. Its purpose to make us burp is now gone ;>(...

This loss of fizz applies to us as well. Sometimes we go so hard to fight the good fight and when it is all said and done we are left feeling void and out of "fizz". We are now unable to serve out our purpose because we are soooo... The "T" word.

(Tired will be referred to as the "T" word because it is dangerous; we over or misuse it and the feeling of the "T" word is definitely contagious.)

Most of time we are not tired just unfulfilled and dissatisfied with our current state; know the difference ;>)!!!!

Remember how you felt the first time you drank a fizz-less soda most of us would say yes and Yuk. LOL

Nobody really enjoys an old, flat, syrupy, soda :>)!!!! LOL

64-GPS (God Positioning System)

Friend In Your Pocket

Save your fizz for yourself; use praise and inspiration as a "Spiritual Burp" Oh what a feeling!

You have purpose.

Friend In Your Pocket

<u>Use Your Mighty Sword ;>)</u>

Today let us start to live through quotes, prose, scripture, and inspiring anecdotals; these tools have helped me to make it this far, and if you my friend allow yourself to be open to receive, these tools will help you as well.

Make a conscious decision to inspire others with your sword (words in reverse) and actions. Realize that your sword is powerful however the spirit behind it is far stronger.

Always speak from your best intentions.

May we all use our breath to utter positivity for it gives rise to Hope and Hope gives rise to new Life. Let us build a New Nation of, Hopers,

66-GPS (God Positioning System)

Friend In Your Pocket

Givers, Teachers, and Students that are not afraid to learn and teach etc.

Positivity birthed from negativity is the "Trending Topic" everyday.

Fuel Your Dreams

In order for a dream to be put in motion it needs wheels for support, the body for structure, a fuel source for movement, and "You" to point it in the right direction while keeping a steady pace.

Have you ever noticed that when you are on the verge of achieving a great dream come true you can't sleep ;>????

While I was writing this book I could not sleeeep, my dream was waking me up at the same time every day, reminding me that I had to keep moving with no stopping until the dream had come to fruition. The spirit of my dream would not be denied or ignored not even in my sleeping dreams. And guess what???? I would not be tired because my actions and spiritual strength was my fuel source.

So remember, when you are driving your "Dream Car" keep going you have more than enough fuel for the trip. God has your reserve tank only reserved for you ;>)!!!!

Once you accomplish one dream it turns into a vehicle that moves you from one goal to the next. Dreams are goals that have not come to pass, yet!!!! One dream realized then accomplished will give rise to many more.

Dreams are like egos, once they are inflated they grow bigger and harder to ignore :>)!!!!

69-GPS (God Positioning System)

So eat your "Wheaties" you Olympic Champion you. This game is yours for the taking ;>)!!!!

Steal the ball and take the game winning shot; you can't miss because you are wearing your; "God Goggles" ;>)!!!!

Friend In Your Pocket

As Long As You Long You Will Always Have Passion!!!!

Desire is when you have done everything on your "to do list" yet you have the hunger "to do" more.

You are learning that the passion is in your pursuit.

Are you feeling the inspiration?

I am ;>)!!!!

Shout out to Pastor Johnnie G. McCann Jr. from St. Lukes Baptist Church in the Village of Harlem N.Y.C

71-GPS (God Positioning System)

Please Build My House; I Dare You!!!!

As you go through your day remember...

Sticks and stones may break your bones if they hit you; however if people keep throwing them your way you can build a sturdy home.

Now that's a bargain. Let them be burdened with the heavy lifting while you design the home you are going to live in ;>).

Never underestimate the power of personal choice and the power to choose what you will accept in your personal space.

The Moon Reminder

Seeing the moon in the daytime is to a child seeing an elder. Both are a necessary reminder that night is coming.

May we all do what we need to do before our nightfall...

Time obviously is not sitting around waiting for you to use it, so move while you are still fast enough to run alongside of it.

Friend In Your Pocket

<u>You Will Find Your Way</u>

What do you do when you are lost? Do you ask for directions? Do you find your own way? Or do you use a GPS?

Sometimes you just have to rely on your instincts and when you feel this way, rely on your "God Positioning System". This GPS is reliable and will continuously restore your strength and confidence in yourself. With this GPS you will get back on course and find your way home in the dark through any storm.

This God Positioning System works when all others are still "Rerouting" LOL but only if you let it ;>).

74-GPS (God Positioning System)

<u>Go For It!!!!</u>

What destination are you destined for?

Do you know?

It is obvious you care, so stop fighting greatness and allow, your God to be your personal GPS.

You will never get lost again. Believe God!!!!

75-GPS (God Positioning System)

__Have You Eaten Today?__

A great thought provoking conversation is mental comfort food. It nourishes the spirit, quenches your thirst, and satisfies your hunger. No empty calories here.

When you are hungry "Spiritual Food" or Nourishment in any sense you will start to lose focus, feel sluggish, get headaches, and have an overall feeling of irritability and agitation. To avoid this make sure you do not skip any opportunity to feed your mind, soul, and spirit.

Hunger starts as a thought ;>).

<u>Sign Language</u>

Conversations with the most high often happen in silence.

"Peace be Still"

Your greatest "Life Altering" and "Soul Stirring" conversations will take place with no spoken words and an overwhelming feeling of urgency that only "You" will feel and hear. They say Bad Boys move in silence and God is the "Ultimate Bad Boy". He assembles his army in silence but his mighty "Victory Thunder" is loud, bright, and clear.

Do not worry; you have not "Crazy" God is working with you on your strategic plan just listen ;>).

77-GPS (God Positioning System)

Silence is sometimes the only way to show your gratitude~ George Washington

<u>What Are You Talking To;>)????</u>

Speak Life into your Thoughts, Desires, Dreams, and Aspirations to Promote Growth, Completion, and Success.

Speaking to deficits fosters Stagnation and Spiritual death.

Start a Spiritual, Gratitude, or Inspirational Journal

Chronicle the episodes of life that make you feel grateful and keep you inspired.

When there is nothing new on your network reruns of Hope are, "Oldies but Goodies" ;>)!!!!

79-GPS (God Positioning System)

<u>Are You In Season ;>)????</u>

I was once called a "Late Bloomer" I was offended, I was hurt, I believed I was already a head of my time. (So I believed).

One day while gardening I was trimming dead flowers; I was marveled and pleased to find a bunch of freshly blooming flowers underneath the dead ones.

They rose from the ashes like the "Phoenix". In that moment, "Late Bloomer" was so befitting. They stole the show and reminded me that our season is over when we decide.

This refreshing discovery made me say I don't mind being a "Late Bloomer". Blooming at the appointed time will make someone's

80-GPS (God Positioning System)

day and fill it with the unexpected. It is never too late to bust through the gate!!!!

Better late than never ;>)!!!! May "We" be in bloom long after our, "So-Called" season has ended.

Ask Yourself…

Would you rather struggle as a child or would you rather struggle as an adult?

If you had to choose whether you could be wealthy as a young adult vs. an adult what would be your answer?

Who lasts longer the early riser or the late bloomer? What lasts longer the Super Nova or the North Star?

As You Already Know I am Fine with being a, "Late Bloomer" ;>)

81-GPS (God Positioning System)

<u>You Can Do It;>)!!!!</u>

As you work or go about your daily routine today remember you are doing your best. You are better than you were last year on this very day.

Believe you can do better; Next year you will be better than today.

However if you find you are no better or even worse off than last year, know that acknowledgement is the first step to recovery.

As long as you have breath in your lungs you have an opportunity to change.

Come on, "You Can Do Itttt" ;>)!!!! Thanks Adam Sandler.

<u>Use Trauma To Survive</u>

Survivors coping with "Post Traumatic Stress"; first realize they are experiencing this disorder after they have made it through a bad situation or rough ordeal.

Confront the trauma. How does it make you feel? What happened?

Deal with the feelings everyday (intentionally) until each day is better than the last.

Recognize your purpose and the lessons learned.

You were spared for a divine reason.

You are important and matter to our universe.

Friend In Your Pocket

Pull yourself out of despair, dust yourself off, give Thanks and Praise for Victory and for closure share your testimony with someone else in need.

Testimony gives us a renewed purpose.

We are winning again in spite of our, "So Called" defeat ;>)!!!!

<u>Are You Using Your Degree, Yet ;>/????</u>

Reflect on your past. No need to stress over it.

Learn and Teach from your unique Lesson Plan.

Somewhere someone needs your Guidance.

Survivors should only feel guilty if they do not help others through their experiences.

Remember we are all teachers because we have learnt.

I received my Degree from the University of, "Hard Knocks".

Where did you receive your Degree from????

85-GPS (God Positioning System)

The Storm That Brought The Calm

Ok it's sharing time.........

We all have a story so here is one of mine based on a traumatic event in my life.

Tensions are running high. I was being cursed at violated, and mistreated. "Can I make a phone call?"

"I can't see, I can't breathe. I need medical attention" I exclaimed.

"Shut up and close your eyes", a police officer replied. As I sat freezing in a cell with 3 Latinas accused of drunk driving, only worried about what their parents were going to say.

86-GPS (God Positioning System)

Friend In Your Pocket

As other officers walked past shaking their heads and saying to one another, "that's her?" I sat in pain and in fear.

Just then and angelic voice vibrated through the dank airy cell. "Open this cell, she has been here since 8:30 pm and its 1 am, "ma'am we are going to the hospital."

The police officers stood at attention and scrambled to come up with a legitimate reason why I sat here in this condition. Ridiculous reasons like the phones were busy and we tried calling several times. The EMT was not convinced as she looked at my pepper sprayed stained face and battered wrist which sustained "cuff burns," a condition I had never heard of before this night.

87-GPS (God Positioning System)

Friend In Your Pocket

The EMT assured me that I would be fine and I believed her (her kindness I will never forget).

I was then transported to the hospital but not before I was paraded around the precinct in shackles on my hands, waist, and feet. I was handled with less dignity than an animal.

I was ashamed of the woman I was at this moment.

The ambulance ride was the safest I would feel throughout this ordeal. When you are brought into a hospital shackled like a wild unruly beast the public psychologically associates you as such. You are prejudged and treated like a bad person, a threat to society. This collective thought process would render me inferior

88-GPS (God Positioning System)

medical treatment and I was sent back to the precinct where this nightmare begun.

All I wanted to know was where was my 13-year-old son? Was he okay? Was he alone? I would later learn that he was given to my mother and no charges were filed against him.

My son was the reason why we ended our evening this way. Answers would begin to fill my head along with questions.

If he was innocent, why was he hand cuffed? Why did my asking "why" cause such an outpouring of violence for it all to end with him being charged with nothing?

This made it clear to me that I was the intended target all along.

89-GPS (God Positioning System)

Friend In Your Pocket

While sitting in my cell with my
cellmate, a lesbian named "Tray,
who assured me I was going home
on Monday (and this was only
Friday). I realized this was real and I
had to make sense of what was
taking place. I quickly began to think
of all the civil rights leaders falsely
accused. I reveled in the fact that Dr.
King, Medgar Evans, Malcolm X,
Gandhi, Rosa Parks, Al Sharpton,
Jesse Jackson, Dick Gregory, and
most importantly JESUS had all
found themselves in similar
situations.

Situations where we are trying to
rationalize and reason with
unreasonable people can turn into
violent episodes and unwarranted
mistreatment.

90-GPS (God Positioning System)

Friend In Your Pocket

Some people are unwilling to treat others as people of equal value.

What times in your life made you feel this way????

Thinking in this way allowed me to begin to process all that had taken place.

I had no idea that these actions would be the building blocks to change my spirit forever. Out of this deep pain and tribulation my spirit was awakened. It opened chambers of my Heart, which allowed Agape (unconditional love) and Forgiveness overflow. It forced me to me to look at life through a different lens. I would no longer place blame, hold grudges, and love conditionally. I wrestled with this concept because

91-GPS (God Positioning System)

some people had been rotten to me but yet I "Forgave and Prayed" for them (even the officer who attacked me).

Was I going soft? Was I a punk? Was I a fool? No, I was embarking on freedom. Freedom to love; regardless of reciprocity, was happening to me.

I had lost mental weight and gained spiritual wisdom that many around me had not possessed or had seen. I would often be taken for a fool and miss understood because of my beliefs.

A part of JESUS' story was now my own. I had the dignity to face my persecutors with the knowledge they meant to cause me harm with but instead I would love them despite their actions.

This is the Element of Freedom ;>)!!!! (Thanks Alicia Keys)

Believe GOD is keeping score so that you don't have to. This is not our battle it's the LORDS.

Knowing this I vowed to no longer burden my spirit with the LORD'S work.

No one should be allowed to take up space in your mind. We have so much wisdom to gain and experiences to gather, your mind is prime real estate and has to be protected from squatters and space invaders.

Friend In Your Pocket

Quite a few "Super Bowls" have passed since the "Super Bowl" weekend of 2008 but it will never be forgotten.

Over a year went by and the tears still fell, the pain was still there.

On March 5, 2009 I was acquitted on all counts.

Once the judge heard all witness accounts from me and the officers involved he was compelled to rule in my favor. It was an added bonus that the officer had the gall to admit to using unnecessary force without provocation and remorse. This testimony would exonerate me and grant me victory legally, civilly, and morally in the court of public opinion.

94-GPS (God Positioning System)

Friend In Your Pocket

The courtroom would erupt in JOY when the verdict was rendered.

Supporters and Strangers would come from near and far in hopes that justice would be served, and that day we all won.

Sure the fight for civil rights and equal rights for all rolls on and the mental scars are still present, however all of this adds to my thirst for spirituality and my love for GOD has increased.

In regards to this experience I thank all of my Persecutors for killing the old me and allowing GOD to make me over.

The site of death for one situation is the birthplace of a new and improved way of life.

95-GPS (God Positioning System)

Friend In Your Pocket

I am grateful for being awakened and enlightened.

By any means necessary ;>)!!!!

God knows what will motivate you.

96-GPS (God Positioning System)

<u>Your In Good Company *:>)!!!!*</u>

Having good company on a spirit filled journey usually happens when you're alone. While walking with good spirits you may find yourself in dark places however trusting GOD allows you to have belief that our good spirits will guide you through the dark into the light of your purpose.

Walking with bad spirits allows you to dwell in the dark places without a way out.

<u>Sanctuary is Where the Spirit Is</u>
<u>*;>)!!!!*</u>

Make your mind a sanctuary

When your physical surroundings resemble purgatory

Mental safety is as important as physical safety.

Design a "Panic Room" for your mind.

Joy, Imagination, Creativity, and Positive Thoughts are the Strong Eco-Friendly building materials you will need to construct your luxury "Mental Panic Room" ;>)!!!!

<u>S.T.O.P!!!!</u>

Stop letting...

Stress

Take

Over

Progress

Only if you allow it to!!!!

Stress is a lethal distraction and deterrent to those seeking a stronger sense of self. Stress knows that it robs us of hope; it takes over progress and replaces it with stagnation and despair.

Stop letting S.T.O.P Stop You!!!!

Commit to lightening your load.

99-GPS (God Positioning System)

Friend In Your Pocket

It's OK to put your, "Super Person Cape" in the cleaners every now and then.

100-GPS (God Positioning System)

Friend In Your Pocket

<u>Never Waste Wise Words On Deaf Ears, Show Them With Your Actions!!!!</u>

Never ask of people what you would not do.

You have to show em' with your actions!!!!

And if they don't follow find a new audience!!!!

I know this is easier said than done especially when it comes down to our love ones.

However in the wise words of Gandhi "Be the change you want to see in the world today". Eventually "your world" will catch on.

Believe...

101-GPS (God Positioning System)

<u>Will There Be Blood or Will There Be Joy;>/????</u>

Remember, the battle is not yours!!!!

Are you a trained fighter? Did you aspire to fight everyday of your life?

If not then why are you wearing Gladiator attire? Some of us are "Hyper-Vigilant" ready to react to any supposed threat to our ego. We have those, "Ready for Anything" Spirits. What if we are ready for what never comes to past? We are wasting energy and time. We will never be able to recapture those lost moments in time that could have been better spent do something more positive.

Friend In Your Pocket

Let me see if I can get an "Amen Corner" with this elementary school flashback ;>)...

Do you remember when you were back in elementary school and you were told that someone was going to fight you afterschool? You learned of this bout through the school rumor mill and now you are anxious and terrified as you await three o'clock. God forbid you were in the same class with your contender because when you looked back at them they would taunt you by pounding their fist in the palm of their hand while giving you the evil eye. Geeshhhh I couldn't stand days like this. #StopTheBullying

Sometimes the fight actually happened but if you were fortunate

103-GPS (God Positioning System)

an adult would find out and postpone the fight. These were days when you appreciated nosey adults LOL ;>). Those really were still the good ole days ;>).

The point that I am making here is: What if you kept waiting for the fight at three o'clock and three o'clock never came?

You must lay down your sword and shield, wave the white flag and give the battle over to the LORD. Any relationship, friendship, career etc. That makes you feel that three o'clock feeling or requires fighting, as a prerequisite is not worth the pain, period!!!!

JOY is your birthright not a luxury. No fighting required

<u>Testing Anxiety</u>

Speaking of school, telling the previous story allowed me to conjure up this visualization. Let me see if you have ever had the same feeling… ;>)????

Do you remember taking a test and you look around and start seeing your classmates finishing or turning in their test? How did that make you feel? Did you feel like you wanted to bust out of your seat, or like you had to pee really bad? Did you want to play enee meanie minee moe and just start randomly answering the questions in order to be in the clique of the kids that were finished first? No one wants to feel left behind or be the last person to finish the test.

Friend In Your Pocket

(The last person to finish the test is a rotten egg LOL).

I remember turning in my test early just to be the first person to finish and my grade sucked. From that point on I took testing, school, and timing really serious. I decided to run my own race, wear blinders, and win the race on my own terms.

I was victorious in school and I carried this experience with me as I traveled through life.

Life is not a race take your time. On this divine obstacle course called life everyone who crosses the finish line is a winner. No rotten eggs over here just #Winners ;>)!!!!

Remember those little red, blue, green, and gold stars in school that we worked so hard to get daily? Well that is life eventually every one of us will get our star, when we have earned it.

But Wait!!!! I almost forgot to tell you about the people that finished their test first. Most of them weren't even all that smart and they didn't always get good grades. They just looked smart. Beware of how you perceive people and things you could be idolizing a perception and not the truth.

Friend In Your Pocket

__Forgive and Forget?__

Once we truly forgive there is no need to forget. Over time the negative memories become less trauma filled and fill our lives with wisdom gaining educational value.

If you let it transform from the pesky caterpillar to the majestic butterfly it was born to be.

Believe God Again...

Forgiveness is Our Salvation and the Key to Our Freedom!!!!

Having inner joy allows us to turn the tragic and/or traumatic events of our lives into lessons and sources of inspirations to draw from.

108-GPS (God Positioning System)

Friend In Your Pocket

Let your inner joy rise up through
the storm with the comfort of
knowing this too shall pass.

109-GPS (God Positioning System)

<u>Reading is Fundamental</u>

Never stop reading your book of life because the first chapter was not that great.

The second chapter has great potential to be better, if not let us rewrite our books of life.

Don't ever close the book or quit, just let us find better material to be inspired by and write about.

We must never stop reading and learning. We can create our own "Alternate Endings" It is all about how we maneuver through our Odyssey called, "Life".

Friend In Your Pocket

<u>Where Are Your Keys ;>)????</u>

What is the key to your success?

If you have it then...

OPEN THE DARN DOOR ;>)!!!! LOL

Welcome Home!!!!

We were born perfect and equipped with everything we need to be successful!!!!

Like "Prego" It's in there!!!!

111-GPS (God Positioning System)

<u>Love Your Heart</u>

When our heart is not content it will go outside of itself to find contentment.

Let's find our joy from within so that we do not rely on external validation to feel loved, to love, or be loved.

To thy own self be true~ William Shakespeare

<u>How Much is That Joy In The Window :>)????</u>

Joy needs nothing but faith to thrive and live in our hearts forever.

Happiness requires people, places and lots of things to exist only for a fleeting moment.

You can't buy joy it is priceless ;>)!!!!

<u>Children Are Our Future</u>

I was once a wayward child. I did things that were not becoming of a minor, I drank, had sex before marriage, I was a teen mom, I was failing in school, I was very close to being a loser and deviating off of the path of righteousness forever. In my darkest hours I remembered the pain I felt when my parents were not at their best, then I also remembered all the lessons that were taught to me when they were at their best. This is what changed me, the lessons that I had learned along the way prior to the state that I was in. On my own with God in my heart I had to draw on my past experiences and allow God to guide me back on track, "Blessings in the lessons".

114-GPS (God Positioning System)

Friend In Your Pocket

It is no doubt that our children give us the biggest joys and disappointments. This relationship is nothing short of "Heart Attack Material". Through it all, the lessons that our children teach us is all about never giving up on hope and never stop persevering.

We shall never give up on ourselves or lose sight of our dreams; no matter how murky the waters of life may get we must navigate through it.

Our children will respect us more for doing so.

We must set a strong foundation on fertile soil and GOD will do the rest.

What seeds we sow shall flourish and at harvest time we shall reap; at the appointed time.

115-GPS (God Positioning System)

Friend In Your Pocket

Be patient.

Once we have raised our children
their fate is in their hands.

We have done our best!!!!

Let the miracles unfold ;>).

Don't Be Afraid of The Dark

Inspiration is the light that comes from darkness.

Let us be afraid of the dark no longer.

When we go through rough times in our lives or we watch our loved ones struggle it is important to receive the message out of those tribulations. What are we suppose to learn? Why is this happening? How will we make it through?

I think back to my childhood as I write this and I learned through some of my darkest periods to: stay away from drugs, go all the way in school, don't depend on anyone to pay your way, make sure everyone in my life knows that they are loved no matter the circumstance, look strong even when I am weak, understand my problems and realize the way I solve my problems will affect others, respect is earned, watch over your children with hawk vision, encourage children to shoot for the stars even the ones they can't see, seek help when you need it, share your life experiences with others so that they know they are not alone, be the best you possible, love your differences, love yourself, submit to spirituality, and have faith!!!!

I learned so much more from the mistakes of my parents and I want to thank them for bestowing this responsibility on me because now I can and will encourage others ;>)!!!!

118-GPS (God Positioning System)

Friend In Your Pocket

Of course as I was learning these lessons in my parent's classroom the test was difficult but I passed and now I am a professor in my own lecture hall of, "My Life University".

<u>Hey, Put That Back ;>)!!!!</u>

I do not like when people move my belongings around and they are not as I left them. Friend, how do you feel when this happens to you?

Case and Point in the work place we often have to share space with others; in my circumstance I had my own office but my work friends enjoyed coming in there and working when I was off; they told me they would use my office because it was clean, organized, and smelled good. That was flattering since they had their own office but anyway, I could always tell when someone was using my space because the chairs would be out of place, my plug-in air freshener would be plugged in upside down (causing my sweet

120-GPS (God Positioning System)

smelling oil to spill out on the floor), papers would be strewn about, and basically all of the reasons they gave me for enjoying my space was all the things that they destroyed.

Did they really admire my office? Why did they want to alter my surroundings and what was the purpose?

Sometimes the very thing or things that people claim they like most about you is the thing that they would love to take from you; envy.

I continued to keep my office clean, organized, and smelling good. I would pout when they messed my office up, however I just kept living the way I choose to and refused to be changed by other people's actions.

121-GPS (God Positioning System)

And guess what they started to keep their offices clean, organized, smelling good, and of course they continued to use my office occasionally but these visits diminished. All was well in the world because I stood my ground and did not compromise my values ;>).

Friends remember to... Leave people and things the way you found them. If you must alter the surroundings of others make sure to leave them better than when you found them.

<u>Do You Wanna Dance ;>????</u>

The more we help certain people the more they dislike and grow to resent us.

So when they ask you to dance with them yet again respectfully decline and tell them find another dancing partner.

Sometimes the line between rescuer and persecutor can get confused. Those people in our lives who do not show gratitude, have not learned from their mistakes, and are always in crisis, need time to figure out who is who.

Let's remember to...

Love everyone even the ones who keep stepping on our feet ;>)!!!!

123-GPS (God Positioning System)

However we have the right to decline their invitations to dance. We can say, "No" and still love that person but we must always love ourselves more.

A little "No" won't hurt in this land of plenty; it is necessary.

<u>Your Actions Are Art Too ;>)!!!!</u>

Use the art of persuasion for positive purposes. Society suggests that peer pressure is powerful and the blame for most of the negativity in the world. Imagine if peer pressure was used correctly.

Let's pressure each other to strive to be the best we can be; if we apply constant pressure eventually something will pop.

In this world where all of the images are telling us to; use drugs because we will have fun, alter our bodies because we are not good enough, education is not important because we won't find a job anyway, it's ok to disrespect our fellow brothers and sisters because they will to continue love us anyway, this generation of children are not the future, morals, values and ethics are old fashion and we don't need them, and history is history and has no bearing on our present. Those of us that know better must change the game and pressure our people to not buy into this delusion.

If we continue to apply positive pressure, change won't be immediate but it will be inevitable.

<u>This Is Not a Bill Collector</u>

Ring, Ring, Ring...

Destiny is calling. What do we do? Do we answer the phone or send your destiny to voicemail?

Answer the phone ;>)!!!!

Some of us duck our call to our divine destiny like an annoying bill collector.

Like with all calls where we are required to take action and pay up and make good on a debt they seem annoying but once you answer the call you know exactly what to say and do ;>)!!!!

If feels so much better when you are debt free and when the phone rings it is an opportunity calling rather than an old debt. Stop running from your destiny you deserve to live a better life. You may not like what you have to do to get there but once you arrive there you will enjoy your stay. All you have to do is answer the phone and listen to what God has to say.

You have one more ring before it is too late.

Friend In Your Pocket

<u>Take Those Fun House Mirror Glasses Off!!!!</u>

We live in a delusional society. Some of us are delusional about ourselves, our finances, our relationships, our friendships, our careers, etc.

If we do not like what we see in the mirror which is metaphorically our surroundings, guess what???? We look bad too; we are a part of the reflection.

The best part of stepping out of the delusion is that we know better and with God's help and courage we will assuredly do better.

Thanks Dr. Maya Angelou and Oprah ;>)!!!

129-GPS (God Positioning System)

Friend In Your Pocket

Keep your chin held high; you are on
your way to a better you
acknowledgement is the first step to
recovery <3

It Is Just You and The Shifter; Changing Gears ;>)!!!!

When you are shifting the journey is done without physical company. It seems daunting at first but when we realize the Lord never leaves us alone we feel comforted.

Being alone can be a Spiritual fast for the soul if you are open to receive the message.

This reminds me of a quote I so love by Andre Gide...

"Man cannot discover new oceans unless he has the courage to lose sight of the shore."

Let's discover ourselves without the distractions of others, they will be there when you return and if they are not, they were never a part of the long term voyage; they were just a port stop on our journey.

And it is all, "Good" ;>)!!!!

<u>What is a Safe Risk, Really ;>/????</u>

Living life safely to play it safe and living risky to feel safe; they are both one in the same.

Take positive risks to maximize growth and satisfaction. This will minimize complacency and the risk of having a life with limitations.

Case and point I know a lot of people who are out to make a quick buck because they have bills as well as general wants and needs. However this quick buck could mean putting your life and freedom in jeopardy.

Then on the other hand I know people that live small nonexistent lives because they are afraid to make a positive risk; like marching into boss's office and demanding to know why they have not been promoted in over 10 years; not to mention the fact that they have trained all the people whom have gotten promotions over them.

These two groups of individuals are the same making sacrifices they do not have, to have a false sense of security.

Take a risk for yourself and you will find it was not a negative risk at all. Your "Real Life" was just waiting for you to make your mind and stop playing around with your future.

If you want to be in a position where joy, money, self-esteem, self-worth, etc. is not an object remember this bible verse, "We step out on faith

and not by sight" (2 Corinthians 5:7).
Put your faith first.

Powerful concept!!!!

<u>Deep and High At The Same Time</u>

The Deeper we go into Our Faith the Higher We Ascend.

How Ironic is That ;>) <3????!!!!

It is like planting a tree; the deeper the roots, the taller and stronger the tree will grow.

"So Glad We Made It, We Made It Through" <3

Thank You Pastor Marvin Sapp

<u>Dream With Big Intention, Always :>)!!!!</u>

He who comes to the Lord asking for small things will receive small things in return; He who dreams small will certainly have a small life.

Dream Big, Achieve Your Goals, and Live Large with God *<3*

<u>Live Life L'ive; The Cameras Are Always Rolling ;>)!!!!</u>

Living on this world stage called life we have to remember that when we mess up or miss a step we have to get back up and make the mistake look as though it was intentional.

This was a lesson I learned in the 5th grade while attending C.I.S. 229. I was trying out for a popular dance class and during the audition I missed a step, so I stopped because I was disappointed in myself. As the routine went on I got back into the rhythm but it was too late and I was cut from the dance troop despite being a great dancer. I later asked the teacher why wasn't I chosen and she simply said because you gave up, you are suppose to keep going no matter what.

Wow that hurt, but as I got older I realized she dropped a jewel on me that I would wear for the rest of my life.

Let's master the art of turning our mistakes into our next and best moves.

Thanks Ms. Robinson this brief friendship would help cultivate my life ;>)!!!!

Reality TV

Live your life like you are on live television or streaming live. Either way there is no such thing as, "Another Take" or a "Do Over". When you don't have a choice you will rise to your full potential and render a flawless presentation.

Sure there is a chance that you may say or do the wrong thing, at the wrong time. However as long as you keep going and give more perfection than flaws it will not make a difference in the long run.

Let me give you an example…

I love watching figure skating. It feels awesome when someone gives a flawless performance but do you ever notice the performances that looked flawless to you did not get a perfect ten? Then you notice another skater had a better technical performance that was more challenging than the last but they fall during the performance; your heart sinks for them as they await their score. To your surprise as well as the skater they get a better score than the person that had the flawless performance.

Ask yourself why is that?

The answer is perseverance; this person although there triple Sal chow or triple axel seemed nearly impossible they attempted to do it anyway and did their best. This counts more than someone who did

not take a risk and had a flawless
performance.

When I was younger it seemed unfair
but as I got older I realized that this
is just life.

<u>The devil Can Play Baseball Too</u>
<u>;>/!!!!</u>

The curve balls from hell will always come when you are at the top of your game or at the bottom of the ninth. Just know this and armor yourself accordingly, evil will be struck out.

Lean on the word of the Lord and count on Joy.

You will make to the home stretch>)!!!!

<u>Do You Rise or Fall ;>/????</u>

Joy rises in the face of adversity. It is a gift from God to be joyful in spite of and despite of your current state of adversity.

Joy is like the heat; it rises

Happiness is like the cold it falls.

Count on joy and not happiness; for joy is organic and happiness is a man-made synthetic aka unreliable. LOL ;>)!!!!

__Invention is Birthed From Needs__

Struggle is the mother of invention. Everything in this world was created because someone before us needed it.

Every component created gives rise to a new set of struggles and a new set of needs.

The lesson here...

Either create something that is always a necessity or be the person that is able to fix the things we cannot live without.

<u>Are You Audit Proof;>????</u>

Can your life stand an internal or external audit?

We get so wrapped up at work and home making sure everyone's files of life are neat, legible and audit proof. That we tend to forget about ourselves.

Let's vow to ourselves that we will be a better bookkeeper for our souls.

Whether we face an internal or external audit you will not fail or have to write a corrective action plan.

It is not too late to do a self-audit and make the necessary revisions before our books become a matter of public record.

146-GPS (God Positioning System)

Friend In Your Pocket

Go for it, it always seems worst than
it really is ;>).

147-GPS (God Positioning System)

<u>It Is Your Own Fault</u>

We teach people how to treat us with our actions. We must treat ourselves well and stay consistent. Anyone wishing to be in our circle will have no choice but to do the same.

If they refuse they have no right to take up physical and mental space in our life.

Remember the outcome depends on our actions.

Stop enabling "Spiritual and Emotional Leeches"!!!!

We get sucked dry while they get fat off of our blood. Wowwww!!!!

Friend In Your Pocket

Now where they do that at :>????
This makes no sense does it;>????

Change the Game...

<u>Gift Yourself</u>

Forgive more and regret less; everything is in accordance to God's plan.

S.T.O.P (Stress Takes Over Progress) holding on to dead things for fear of what others think. That season has simply ended. So when people ask you about a friend, girlfriend/boyfriend, job, address, etc. that is no longer, tell them...

"That season has ended" Then continue to move on to "Your" regular scheduled programming ;>)!!!!

"The Battle is Not Yours" Thanks Yolanda Adams (Gospel Singer) for Reminding Us All.

<u>Ability is So Underrated These Days!!!!</u>

Be grateful for the ability to be "Able To", pay bills, get bills, have a career, have life regardless of your health etc. The things that seem like nuisances in our life should be celebrated as well as the things that make us joyful.

The gift of feeling or affect is under rated; when we lose these gifts is when the real issues start.

Being, "Able To" is a gift and if we are not able to at this time I have no doubt that we will find a way to be able to the next time.

All of our nuisances should be motivation to make these things a

Friend In Your Pocket

"Non Factor" the next go round (Hi Evelyn from BBW Miami ;>)!!!!

Be motivated by adversity!!!!

Are we safe within ourselves?

Let's make ourselves a Sanctuary.

<u>Are We Giving Thanks or Being Thankful To Take ;>/????</u>

Thanksgiving as a metaphor,

What are we bringing to the feasting table of life? What is our contribution? Do we come to the table baring gifts of food or do you come with Tupperware? LOL

But seriously how are we impacting our world? Are we squatters living off the fat of the land or are we helping run the family farm that feeds the nation.

I won't even tell you what side we should be on; I know that you have figured this out by this time and if you haven't... Start reading this book from the beginning again LOL ;>)!!!!

153-GPS (God Positioning System)

Friend In Your Pocket

Acknowledgment is the first step to recovery.

Napoleon Hill said it best...

"Victory usually comes in disguise of a misfortune or temporary defeat"

You have victory in your so-called defeat ;>)!!!!

Friend In Your Pocket

<u>Use Your Platform to Uplift</u>

Social Media and Music is a Blessing ;>)!!!!

However if you are not using your platform for the sake of positivity and uplifting your peers, you are not part of the problem.

You Are The Problem!!!!How Are We Inspiring One Another :>/????

Please Don't Kill My Positive Spiritual Vibe High by Dragging Me Down; with Negativity and Vulgarity.

Those Things are such a Joy Buzz Killer ;>)!!!!

Thanks Kendrick Lamar (Hip Hop Artist)

155-GPS (God Positioning System)

What Seasoning Is...

When not used properly "Seasons of Favor" do not last long. So ask yourself... Am I ready? You are up next.

This is what I believe happens to people whom rise to stardom; they have dreams to be the next this or the next that; then when they achieve their initial goal they do not know what to do next.

So they start doing things out of their normal character, they make poor choices, they become open to negativity, and they become someone else. Sadly, they set out to become some else all along and this is why it is so important to have a strong sense of "Self", you won't be swayed off of your path. The moment you chose someone else's path was the moment you made your first big mistake.

Have "Your" plan ready when you open the window to witness your "Season of Favor". When you are sure, jump and your plan will act like your safety net.

Trust and believe in "Yourself"

To try is to fail.

If you don't plan, plan to fail.

Some people don't know how to love.

Be that person that doesn't know how to hate ;>).

Friend In Your Pocket

Money can buy momentary love and
happiness but it can't buy self worth
and joy, which are gifts from God
and we all know gifts given not
bought ;>)...

Joy Bullies

Negative people often attempt to mess with a joyful persons walk; they try to make joyful people mirror their negative images.

When this happens we have to remind those people...

"Don't be confused by our sunshine because we can also bring a thunderstorm, if we wanted to however we choose joy ;>)!!!!

Let's drench those weeds with a good ole sun shower and pray they show us their flowers.

Creating boundaries and guard rails are important on this highway to joy ;>)!!!!

159-GPS (God Positioning System)

<u>Who is Sleeping On Your Sofa</u> <u>;>)????</u>

I recently discovered the phenomenon called, "Couch Surfing" this is when someone joins a web-based community of people that are interested in seeing how the other side lives. When they muster up enough courage to come to your town and bunk with a total stranger for a period time agreed upon prior to their visit, some say this is safer and cleaner than going to a hostel.

A good friend of mine and me were in Central Park with her daughter enjoying the first signs of spring when a motley crew of three introduced themselves to us. My friend and I had noticed the threesome playing the guitar singing and laughing as if they had known each other for quite some time. As the group approached, the Jewish male in this group from Williamsburg Brooklyn asked if he could ask me a question and I said, "Sure" He asked me what made me so happy and stated that he could see my joy from across the lawn. I smiled and told him life made me feel that way. God, the good, the better, and the unspeakable brought me joy. He smiled and the group joined my friend and I on our blanket. Later I would be introduced to the songbird with the guitar whom was a pretty African girl from France she was also part Madagascar; she would sing a beautiful song for us having to do with being a stranger in her own home (which was beautiful). Than we would come to know a beautiful Malaysian girl who was here and her parents thought she was here visiting a close friend. The Malaysian girl told us that in order to go on a first date in Malaysia you had to know your suitor for at least six months before you could be asked to go on a date, a custom which she practiced. We would all laugh at her for sleeping on a complete stranger's couch but yet she was unwilling to change her dating rules, (LOL) the irony. The Jewish male would later tell me that he was embarking on a spiritual journey where his GPS (God Positioning System) will lead him to South East

Friend In Your Pocket

Asia; he would leave three weeks later to set out to achieve his goal of being joyful everyday of his life and to do whatever makes him feel that way every day of his life moving forward, pretty ambitious right? But you must understand he has that good ole faith power and with that you cannot lose.

Later in this encounter we all would dance the Jewish dance the "Hora" in the middle of Central Park, and we were complete strangers no more.

Leaving this encounter I saw the necessity for Couch Surfing when done properly. I was blessed to be a part of this moment in time.

I keep in touch with my Couch Surfers to this day, thus proving that friendship can bloom anywhere and anytime, if you are open to the experience ;>).

<u>Can I Help You ;>????</u>

Necessity has no ego.

Want or desire is attached to pride. Bottom line is, a closed mouth won't get fed.

So if you are in need and not in want, you will not take "No" for an answer.

Discern whether the thing you desire is a need or a want then follow this

Yugoslavian Proverb...

"Complain to someone who can help you."

<u>Build A-Friend</u>

Keep in mind that you can't make
friends. Parents stop telling your
children to make friends. I used to
work in Head Start for many years
and I remember talking to children
daily that were either crying or
pouting with their arms crossed on
their chest saying, "She/He" won't be
my friend!" And do you know why?
Because they were taught that they
can make friends. The truth is that
you can't make a friend like you
make perfect cookies or the perfect
PB and J (Peanut Nut Butter and
Jelly), we have to grow and cultivate
friendships like those of us who
garden do.

Friend In Your Pocket

We must teach to look as friendships in this manner and not the notion that you can make a friend like build a bear ;>).

Reality is you can't make anyone do anything. Remember that.

Making a person be in a friendship is like playing tug of war; someone will wind up with mud in their face ;>)!!!!

Growing and cultivating a friendship is like gardening; we must accept people for who they are and we must understand that some friendships are annual; meaning they come around once in a season and some friendships are perennial they come around every season. This metaphor evokes gratitude and takes away the feeling of entitlement.

This lesson is heartbreaking for children when they learn they can't make friends but even more damaging for adults.

Let us start this new way of thinking early to minimize our adult heartaches.

Ericka Badu said it best...

"Pick my friends like I pick my fruit"

<u>Do Something Different Start a Friend Garden</u>

Friendship can bloom any season.

Go Pick a Friend and Plant It In Your Garden ;>)!!!!

Draw What Your Friend Garden Looks Like Below ;>)!!!!

Never trust the man that tells you all his troubles but keeps you from all his joy

~Jewish Proverb

169-GPS (God Positioning System)

<u>Are You Being Drained and Not Refilled ;>/????</u>

If someone does not think of you when they are having the best time of their lives, they should not be allowed to call on you when their life is in shambles.

We teach people how to treat us remember that.

Ok in this instance I have Two Cases and One point ;>)!!!!

<u>First Case:</u>

I know someone that is always complaining, just always going through... One day I was sad and felt like complaining when I realized out of all of our conversations they had never asked me how I was doing. I was instantly annoyed when I reflected and had an epiphany. I had created this "Emotional and Spiritual Leech" It was my fault and I decided to change my ways. I stopped answering every phone call and when I answered the phone I put a time cap on the amount of time I would spend listening.

I felt wonderful the phone calls subsided. Of course I missed the friendship in the beginning but my life was so peaceful without it.

The best lesson learned was that moving forward all of my conversations were going to be well balanced and nutritional like for food for the soul ;>).

Second Case:

While perusing through any given Social Networking Site you may see some of your supposedly close friends having a blast. They are buying clothes, popping bottles of expensive wines and spirits, eating at the most lavish of places, vacationing, etc. They appear to be having the time of their life and guess what you are not a part of it.

However when they call you they sound down and out, depressed, and complaining about their finances, their new friends, etc. Now you knowwww you are not bugging or going crazy because you know what you saw in their last post or update. Nevertheless you indulge in their latest pity party, you proceed to talk them off the ledge, and assure them things will get better. Then this phone call ends either with them telling you they will call you back later (as you think please don't do me no favors) ;>) or they put you on hold and never return to the other line.

Low and behold this process will continue time after time and what do you do about it? Do you continue to answer the phone and become a free therapist for someone who can obviously afford to pay LOL ;>)?

The Point:

We must commit to reserving our mental and spiritual strength for people who do not abuse our caring nature. And for those of us reading this and you are the "abusive friend" that I am speaking of it is time for you to realize that you have to be grateful for the people who listen and coach you through your darkest hours for those are the people that should enjoy the sunshine with you.

People often attach themselves to strong people (like us) in times of crisis but choose to associate with weak "Non-Contributing" people in times of celebration.

When the phone rings the next time remember that this is your time to commit to reserving your strength, moral support, and encouragement to your friends and family whom appreciate and deserve it <3

Friend In Your Pocket

This time tell them you have to go, see you when I see you (In my Martin Lawrence Voice, for my Martin Fans ;>)!!!!

The honest truth is your life is better without them; you are just hung up on the idea that they have discarded you like a Christmas toy the day after Christmas. Once you get over that rejection you will be fine it is a human emotion that is fleeting. Keep in mind; "Rejection is God's Protection". Thanks Hill Harper ;>)!!!!

A better crop of humans is out there just waiting for us to grow and pick them so go out and enjoy ourselves

I go out all the time by myself and have the best time meeting new

175-GPS (God Positioning System)

people having casual conversations, and most importantly leaving when I want to. It is such a liberating feeling going out on your own terms.

Try this one day, I promise you the more you do it the more you will fall in love with yourself and realize what an awesome person and friend you truly are. And guess what ;>)???? You will become more selective of the friends you allow to enter your personal space.

Promise to try this you owe it to yourself. And if you are someone that is already doing this encourage others to do it.

Your First BFF should always be "You" ;>)!!!!

Point Made ;>)!!!!

176-GPS (God Positioning System)

<u>Are You Seeking Counsel :>/????</u>

A friend should be able to speak on your behalf.

A friend should be a counselor.

A counselor listens, develops strategies, and defends you when necessary. God, Therapist, and Attorneys are also referred to as counselors. If your friend can't advocate on your behalf this friendship is subject to judgment and the sentence is likely to be death.

Let's strive to be counselors and accept nothing less from those around us.

<u>Lottery Gift or Burden</u>

This is just a cute story I wanted to share...

An 81 year old woman just won over 200 Million in the New York State Lottery. One of my friends was enraged and said," What is that old lady going to do with all that money at her age?" She went onto say that someone younger should have won and yada, yada, yada ;>)...

Who are we to second-guess God?

Imagine how this older woman must have felt. She was probably saying why now, after all her life struggles she was being rewarded in the winter of her life???? The reward was coming at a time when she could not fully enjoy the money the way she could have when she was younger. Maybe she did not think this was fair either.

The answer is simple...

When we are younger we tend to waste money, we don't know the value of a dollar, and tend to be poor judges of character.

This woman should made for a better recipient because she will make sure she helps people who are truly in need and she will get to live the rest of her days comfortable and financially stress free.

The bottom line is she must have done something right in her lifetime to receive such a reward.

Friend In Your Pocket

Simply put, God thought she was more qualified for the job ;>)!!!!

We must all accept when we are not qualified for positions that other people are in and not envy them.

It is just simply not our time, yet!!!!

Be patient...

180-GPS (God Positioning System)

Friend In Your Pocket

Don't Stand to Close To The Platform; The Breakthrough Train Is Coming!!!!

How do you know when your breakthrough is coming? When you have put it in your mind, that you are not going to take "No" for an answer, when nothing appears to be working in your favor but yet you have the energy and the spirit to keep going, when all you do is eat, breath, dream, and sleep your breakthrough!!!!

This is when you know, when nothing else matters, when you see yourself in your new role, when you can see a year from today, and your breakthrough has manifested, then you smile because you know it has already been done.

181-GPS (God Positioning System)

Friend In Your Pocket

Wendy Williams coined it best...
"Futuristic Vision" Thanks again to
my, Big Sister Friend in My Head"
;>)!!!!

A divine breakthrough won't let you
fail or forget. All revelations must be
fulfilled as prophesized ;>)!!!!

I believe this and when "You" do the
same chills and goose bumps I
experienced when I wrote this will
become apparent to you, once you
fully believe that this is true for
yourself.

<u>Use The Day To Be Awake</u>

Live out your dreams in the daytime with your eyes open.

Make a vow to stop tossing and turning while you are sleeping and stop sitting around daydreaming when you are awake. Go make something shake ;>)!!!!

From this day forward, while you sleep during the night, don't spend your time dreaming; "REST".

<u>Childlike Soul Searching</u>

Blessed are the pure at heart for they will see the Lord

~Matthew 5:8

My Grandmother Ruth gave this to ponder and I did. The pure at heart is a living being that lives to their full potential with the best of intentions. The pure at heart starts with childhood; when we are children we live fearless we do anything we conceive of doing and say whatever is true even though these things may be hurtful. They do not have the concepts of boundaries and only know how to tell the truth; it is us the adults that teach them how to lie and create limits to their achievements.

Friend In Your Pocket

So if we truly want to be pure at heart we have to take lessons from the youngest children of the world. We must speak the truth and act out any notion we can conceive without fear. That is living to your full potential and having the purest heart. When you treat yourself well; in turn you will treat the world around and beyond with the same respect. There goes that feeling of empathy and notice it starts young; if we build up each other's self-esteem there is no limit to what we can all conceive with pure intentions and pure concepts.

Learning from the ancients is the wise thing to do for, "There is nothing new under Sun". So why do we take issue with learning from our young? They come equipped with all the tools necessary for survival that come from the spirit world unadulterated. There is no shame from learning from the young the shame is if we do not recognize their contribution to our lives. Learn from them and respect their wisdom! We could all learn a thing or two ;>)!!!!

"Don't Waste Wise Words on Deaf Ears; Show Them with Your Actions"

Inspire Others by Your "Movement".

~Qwana Reynolds-Frasier

<u>What Are You Watching ;>/????</u>

One of my guilty pleasures is some of the funniest reality shows on television.

Ok that was my confession I engage in mindless behavior at times!!!!

Well one day while indulging I realized I had turned into a consumer obsessed with other people's lives while I sat and watched my life pass me by.

Our current state is only a pit stop to get fixed, tuned up, and then go win this race.

You can do it; the TV will be there when you get back.

187-GPS (God Positioning System)

Friend In Your Pocket

While the other networks are showing re-runs; let's make sure that our network called; "Self" is always airing new episodes from our every changing new season.

Do You Watch VH1 Like I Do ;>)???? No Not the Cable Network; I am talking about the, "Victorious Holy 1" Network. God-o-Vision for all.

No Television Required.

<u>Who's Driving ;>/????</u>

Push Pass "Your Past" by using "GOD-Given" Forgiveness as your vehicle.

Remember GOD is in control.

Sit in the driver's seat with the gear in cruise. You will be free to receive all of His Wisdom, Love, and Blessings without stepping on the brakes.

What a wonderful visualization ;>).

<u>Don't You Ever Get Too Comfortable!!!!</u>

What great advice (Thanks Lil Wayne for reminding us all). When your life starts feeling like those tight jeans and hard bottom shoes at the dinner table and you begin to undo your zipper and kick off your shoes, then you realize you have on sweats and sneakers. It is time to lose that dead mental weight.

Restless spirits require a makeover where, "You" are your own "Glam Squad." God is your "Anna Wintor" and the Bible replaces Vogue in this fashion world called life.

Make the changes required, walk the catwalk, and then tear down the runway on your own terms ;>)!!!!

190-GPS (God Positioning System)

Friend In Your Pocket

<u>P.U.S.H</u>

Prayer

Ushering in a

Spirit to a

Heavenly State

Push to give rise to your divine right. A Nudge turns into a PUSH when you long to walk in accordance to your faith, however the world around you does not foster mental and spiritual peace.

We need a PUSH to realize our full potential. Ushering our dead spirit to Heaven is the death of our old life in exchange for a new life that has promise of favor and abundance.

191-GPS (God Positioning System)

Friend In Your Pocket

Heaven can be a dream realized.
Heaven could be inner peace.
Heaven is the state of being that is in
accordance with the Lord and His
Divine Plan for our Life.

<u>Are You Broken; Where Do You Belong;>/????</u>

Remember that something or someone broken once belonged to a "Whole". It was once strong when it belonged to a unit.

Can you reunite the broken pieces and put them in their rightful place? Can it be repurposed and used as something else?

When at all possible we should give broken people a new home and a new purpose. However this has to be a mutual agreement.

When people truly want to belong to a strong unit once again they will welcome this opportunity with open arms and vow to never be a broken piece again.

A little P.U.S.H Always helps ;>)!!!!

<u>Celebrate The Birth of Everything!!!!</u>

We often take for granted the luxury of knowing our "birth date". Some of our foremothers and fathers did not have this luxury. This creates such a sense of loss. So when does this person celebrate on some arbitrary date? They will never know what date their mother, sacrificed her physical safety in order to bring them into this world, the date when their mother's life was changed for the better forever.

Knowing the birth date of any event in your life it is important to know. What are the birth dates of, Your "Dreams", "Your Pain", "Your

Joys", "Your Triumphs", and "Your Liberation"?

You should know those dates and cherish each one. The state of your being at the time each one was birthed gives you insight as to why things happened the way that they did.

Of course eight numbers (mm/dd/yyyy) do not represent who you are in totality but it sure feels good to be recognized at an appointed time year after year (unless you're a Leap Year Baby) ;>)!!!! It gives you something to look forward to and plan around or not, if you so choose; the operative word is "choose" because you have the power of, "Choice".

196-GPS (God Positioning System)

Friend In Your Pocket

Not knowing negates your choice.

Choose to know who you are in your entirety. Birthdates and milestones included.

197-GPS (God Positioning System)

Did You Know You Were a Professor;>/????

Experience is the teacher that teaches from the lesson plan you have created. Pay attention in class; school is in session. If you are not dedicating your full undivided attention you will miss information needed for the final exam and you all know it is worth 50 percent of your grade ;>).

Did you realize throughout all your time on this earth that you were teaching yourself? We create our own habits good and bad. Stop and ask yourself "Why?" Often times your answer will surprise you.

So when you are developing the lesson plan for your upcoming semester remember the lessons of classes passed; no need to repeat old information each class should be new and built upon the foundation set prior. All knowledge gained is working towards your degree and you are either going to flunk or graduate top of "Your" class.

You grade your own exam and decide your own educational future!!!!

Friend, we are in full control of what we learn, whom we choose to learn from, and whom we teach.

Let us make every lesson count.

I am so inspired by 'Us"! We are the very best at whatever we believe wholeheartedly we can achieve.

199-GPS (God Positioning System)

Friend In Your Pocket

We are all predisposed to thrive in adverse conditions and come through as pioneers, craftsman, innovators etc. This is no mistake, no anomaly; it is our divine right to claim our place amongst the stars from which we came.

We all must continue to accomplish great feats.

<u>We Are A Work Of Art</u>

We are born blank slates that get painted with knowledge, hurt, joy, desire, defeat, and genetic dispositions. When we see others or ourselves for that matter decline we often jump to ask what is wrong. When we should be focusing on, what happened?

Most of us do not set out or strive to be a loser or become a person who struggles to thrive. This state of being is usually taught or learned.

Either way a canvas can be painted over although the markings of the paintings before lie underneath the surface it is important to make the corrections and move on.

201-GPS (God Positioning System)

Friend In Your Pocket

We are a masterpiece in the making.

Did you know that Leonardo Da Vinci worked on the most recognized portrait in the entire world until he died? It is speculated that he worked on the, "Mona Lisa" for 12-15 years. And if I know any better I would venture to say that if could had did some more tweaking it could have taken longer than that. This is just another example why of, "It ain't over until it is over"

God will "Never" be done with you because He Will "Never" die. Keep the Faith and Work Hard.

Believe God...

202-GPS (God Positioning System)

<u>Check Your Messages</u>

What is the Message in the message...? I was pondering this word and could not get it out my head then God said get it and I said ahhhh got it!!!!

The week prior to the present time I had been so frustrated with the media portrayals of people, news coverage, music videos, lyrical content of music played on the radio, the gang culture exploited and pushed on our children, the gang culture perpetuated by the children in my community and the children I work with everyday.

When you see these things without a filter, smoke and mirrors, and sober; this is overwhelming and you feel like something needs to be done. The message in the word "Message" was we are living in the "Mess-Ages"; a modern day Dark Ages. This appears to be dismal but with hope and faith we must believe that with every Dark Period comes a "Renaissance Period" and a Period of "Enlightenment".

This epiphany; "Friend In Your Pocket" is a gift of word and is living proof that there are people concerned about the direction of the world is going in; and when we ban together we can and will evoke change!!!!

The Mess-Ages are coming to a close... Believe God

Feel Others Pain Without Walking in Their Shoes

I have realized we focus so much on raising children with morals, values, rights, wrong, school, and career. We have to put more emphasis on, "Empathy". We have all gone through so much we tend to give each other basic survival skills but what happens after we survive. We turn out cold and bitter and feel as though if we have "done it" anyone can and this is not true. We forgot to focus on feeling and how seeing other people go through challenges has inspired us to move forward and change our own lives.

My wish is that children grow up with more empathy so that they understand the human spirit of caring for someone other than themselves; this would decrease low self-esteem, an increase of self-esteem will give rise to a decrease of bullying.

People and children who possess empathy are less likely to bully and if less people are the victim of bullying more people will possess high levels of self-esteem.

Pass the gift of empathy; a little goes a long way ;>)!!!!

<u>History is Changed By Forgiveness</u>

Knowing the history of my parents helped me understand and accept their faults; this provoked forgiveness, which gave me permission to Push forward and break the cycle.

Empathy allowed me to humanize my parents.

Forgiveness is your salvation and the beginning of a new life and understanding.

With the grace, eternal and everlasting strength of God, overflowing Joy can turn the most tragic events into valuable lessons and inspiration.

207-GPS (God Positioning System)

Friend In Your Pocket

The Message is in the "Mess-Ages"
ask God what he wants you to know
and he will tell you ,but be prepared
to be forever changed.

Believe wholeheartedly that with
him you can defeat and achieve
anything. Your nights may be long
and dark but your joy and light will
come on the appointed morning; Joy
is on the way.

208-GPS (God Positioning System)

<u>God Is The Captain</u>

Let God be the Captain on every voyage of your life; you might have a few shipwrecks but you will always be saved ;>)!!!!

Whitney Houston sang it best... "When the earth all around me is sinking sand like a solid rock I stand. I go to the rock"

He is the rock that sank the ship and the crew that saved the survivors; sometimes he has to remind us that he is present in our lives.

What Lies Beneath ;>/????

Some of us brush our teeth, floss regularly, go to the dentist, buy veneers, get our teeth whitened, by mouthwash, chew gum, and pop breath mints; then we open our mouths and the stench that spews from us is vile, vulgar, and damaging.

The amount of work, money, time, and energy invested in a clean smile should also be afforded to our souls and spirit.

It is the equivalence to putting on new clothes after working out or playing basketball; we would say ewwww that's nasty, right...?

Ok then let us get it together, stop with the hypocrisy and be consistent.

210-GPS (God Positioning System)

Friend In Your Pocket

Our message has to be in line with
our actions.

211-GPS (God Positioning System)

The Power of Aroma

The power of aroma is understated and taken for granted. We focus on looking a certain way but some of us do not pay attention to the aromas we bring us as well as the aroma we leave behind when we depart.

Take this example literally, figuratively, and spiritually. Bring the aroma that best signifies who you are and what lasting impressions you want people left with when they come in contact with you.

Are you clean like fresh washed clothes, sweet like candy, fragrant like a wild flower, cleaver like clover, and sharp like citrus, brilliant and savory as honey?

Friend In Your Pocket

Or are your aromas pungent like cat pee, creepy like a skunk, or an irritating nuisance like wet pennies?

Let your aroma decide; this is the one true first and lasting impressions. So remember to ask yourself what is my aroma saying about me? Non-verbal communication sets the tone.

I am often told, "You smell so good!" "What are you wearing?" I like to mix my perfume, so I begin to tell whomever all the scents that I have on, I can begin to notice their attention waning and I realize... They want to be in my presence a little while longer to bask in my aroma. They never really cared about the designer; this encounter has allowed them to escape their reality if only for a moment and has altered their state of mind, in a positive way.

So with all things that we enjoy, we love the effect but are not interested in how it works. How many of us have smart/android phones but do not have a clue about how an O/S (Operating System) works? LOL we just care that it works ;>)!!! The darn phone is smarter than its owner LOL. So try maintaining an aroma that best coveys the message you want the public to know; it works ;>)!!!!

214-GPS (God Positioning System)

Behind Closed Doors

The measure of our character is what we do when no one is looking or there is no risk of getting caught.

What do we do when we believe we are alone?

Sometimes we have terrible thoughts, sometimes we have habits no one knows about etc.

What we have to do is train ourselves to act in accordance to all things positive and productive. Just imagine if there was a fly on the wall and the walls could talk what would they be conversing about ;>)!!!!

Just when we think we are alone just remember the entire universe is watching us ;>)!!!! Geeshhhh that is

215-GPS (God Positioning System)

Friend In Your Pocket

a lot of pressure but we must be ready for anything thing at anytime.

Let's Measure our character daily instead of our physical weight sooner or later they will balance each other out ;>)!!!!

Remember change your mind or make it up whatever you do make a choice and make it positive and pure.

What's Really Good ;>)????

What's Good?

This is a question we often ask one another. What is the normal response? Nothing, Chilling, I can't call it etc. Are these responses true? Do we have nothing good in our lives? Are we stagnated just chilling in the refrigerator of life waiting for someone to give our lives meaning?

Did you ever notice you rarely hear; I'm great, everything is good, I am phenomenal!!!

Friend In Your Pocket

I challenge us to respond in this manner. Let's change our responses to change our state of mind, hence changing the world around us.

I believe that is why we all embrace the popular term, "It's All Good!" this phrase states that no matter the situation or circumstance the mere fact that we are still alive makes it "All Good" and it truly is ;>)!!!!

<u>Shining Star</u>

When your light is the brightest
people stop, stare, and take notice.
Believe your strength, your power,
and don't question it. Use it to
achieve your goals.

Ok sharing time...

I am a beautiful full figure black
woman with pink and black hair
(most of the time, I switch my color
but pink is a staple) Needless to say
when I go out in public for over the
last 20 years people stop, stare, and
on occasions have asked to take
pictures with me. Now I used to
attribute it to the hair color because
back when I was wearing pink hair
and name belts no one was doing it.
What I would realize was that they

saw something on me that I didn't see; they saw my "light". I would sometimes go out in just black hair and people would still be looking and yes I would feel so uncomfortable why were they looking? Little children would always look and stare then smile at me. I would always get joy because as long as they weren't crying I knew that I was good LOL ;>). I thought maybe it was just me noticing this phenomenon, but my entire family as well as anyone I was around would notice; and they too would feel uncomfortable for me. I was no celebrity why are people so interested in me?

I know now; when my husband and I are out together we get are always amazed and humbled by people watching us. I truly appreciate the braves ones that actually approach me just to engage me in conversation, and want to genuinely get to know me. This is awesome. I am a blessed human being. What I discovered is that people love confident, joyful people and often want to know what makes you that way.

I am so comfortable now when people stare; because I know now that I provide them with hope. They feel as though that if I can do it (whatever the "If " may be) so can they.

So when people stare at you don't assume that something is wrong with you or that they have a problem with you, more than likely something is "Right With You" and they are basking in your glow; so…

Enjoy, Embrace, and Engage.

Are You Still Growing????

There is a saying that says teenagers sleep a lot because they are having growth spurts.

Thankfully, "Spiritual Growth Spurts" happen at any time; you don't need to sleep to experience them. God prefers you to be awake to witness the miracles he performs ;>).

<u>Fingerprints Are Unique But They Can Be Left All Over</u>

Testimony is unique like a set of fingerprints.

We may go through the same situation but deal with them differently. We may go through the same situation but the lessons that we gather may be different.

The hope is that whatever the lesson, situation, and person is that we realize it is a testimony to be told and shared with others in hopes they too will develop their unique testimony.

There is always someone in need of what you have to share.

224-GPS (God Positioning System)

Friend In Your Pocket

I may not be able to reach them the way I have reached you because we all have our own flair and flavor.

So go and share your spiritual food, someone is hungry for it.

225-GPS (God Positioning System)

Friend In Your Pocket

Permission Slip

Say it along with me now…

I hereby give **(Your Name)**
permission to love without
reciprocity, to forgive without doubt,
to learn without shame or limitation,
to try new things without fear and to,
"Do Me" in the best way possible
every day.

Authorized Signature/Guardian

_____**(Your-Self /Your Name)**

Date **Right Now!!!!**

Go on a "Grown Up" field trip where
finding yourself is the purpose and
the fee is freedom!!!!

And as my Great Grandmother used
to say... "Go On Get;>)!!!!"

226-GPS (God Positioning System)

<u>I Won't Go Back;>)!!!!</u>

A shift, a move usually comes with a sense of doubt, fear, anxiety; we are trying to figure out what is going to come next. You have difficulty pinpointing exactly what you feel or what is happening to you. You do not miss what you left and you do not feel connected to the place you are in currently.

So you go about your day and do your normal activities yet you feel unfulfilled. You can even righteously enjoy your step up, whether it is a promotion a change in residence or an old relationship. But,Why????

I experienced this in October of 2010 when I left my childhood bedroom. The last time I slept there was

227-GPS (God Positioning System)

Friend In Your Pocket

October 26th 2010; on October 27th
2010 my family and I piled into our
lawyers office and claim our piece of
the "American Dream Pie" by
acquiring the deed and mortgage to
our beautiful new home.

We had all we had ever wanted our
whole lives in this moment; so I
thought.

My dreams came true, I got my
mama out the "Hood", got one of my
sons out of harm's way, got my other
son off the couch since he had not
had his own bed in 15 years, my
husband accomplished his five year
plan, five years behind schedule;
however it was completed ;>)!!!! I
gave my younger brother something
to strive for as he reached manhood,
and lifted the load off of my brother

228-GPS (God Positioning System)

and father who had not yet been able to see their dreams come to fruition. I had done it all with grace, humility, perseverance, and pleasure.

However something was missing, something was off and I was uncomfortable in my own home. This home was for everyone yet it was not "My Dream" the fairytale did not end here for me. It was an impersonal gift to me from God. Do not get me wrong this home is a Blessing but God spoke to me and said, "There is more yet to come!!!!" So I kept listening and he said, "Write", give your-self to more people because my spirit was and is uncontainable. The light was all over me inside and out and I was ready to shine on anybody in need of my light

Friend In Your Pocket

You Really Can't Go Back Home...

Man cannot trap light, for light will find its way out and ooze through any orifice given the opportunity to escape. That is what I had become trapped light that was acting like a fugitive searching for a crack in the floor boards I found my destination with my God Positioning System (GPS) and hence, "Friend in Your Pocket" was birthed ;>)!!!!

My experience of leaving the room which I had been in since I was six years old, I raised my children there, all of this from that small room, what memories; good, better, and unspeakable. I found myself realizing the quote, "You can never go back home again" and now it made sense, because that was no longer my home. My spirit had left the place; God had a bigger plan for me, my assignment to take care of my family was fulfilled, my debt was, "Paid in full". It was time for me to spread my wings and get ready for the next chapter of this Odyssey. I never felt so Blessed and Humbled.

God makes no mistakes he put "Us" together for a reason. I am pleased and honored to connect with you. I made a vow that I would be an inspiration to whomever I had the privilege to be in the presence of... You my friend!!!!

Since light cannot be trapped open the doors, windows, and skylights of your heart, body, soul, and spirit; escape and allow yourself to achieve

231-GPS (God Positioning System)

greatness by living to your maximum potential.

This is your, "Now What, What's Next Moment?" You Are, What's Up!!!! No one needs to answer you back, because it begins with you. So start moving forward and never look back to go back but look back to remind yourself how far you have come and how much farther you have left to go. (I know that sounds like a lot but you have already begun this journey ;>) .Vow to not allow yourself to become stagnate again.

<u>Keep On Moving Don't Stop</u>

Why do you think Nomads kept moving around? They went towards their opportunity and refused to wait for it to come around again because they knew their lives depended on it.

Take the steps needed for your breakthrough for it is closer than you think. You have been walking towards your purpose all along

As one of Harlem's Beloved Pastor Johnnie G. McCain preaches, "The Passion is in the Pursuit" and remains that way ;>)!!!!

Continue to speak life to your dreams and goals. Talk about them openly with your friends and family. Oftentimes we get so hung up on saying things like," I don't want to jinx it, I am not going to tell anyone because they might steal my idea" Or, "I won't tell anyone but you " LOL ;>)!!!! The truth is all you need is one "Hater" if that were true.

We tend to give Man too much power; what is for you and given to you by God, no man can take. God defies the odds; believe that more people are rooting for your success than you know. As the good book states, "Know from whence your help cometh" see when you know this and truly believe in his word you will be able to scream your dream from the mountain over better yet over "Social Media Outlets" LOL Like I did; and now look you are reading our "Masterpiece" ;>)!!!!

Friend In Your Pocket

There are benefits of talking about your goals; first it allows you to get used to the idea of your new role. It takes the weirdness out of saying my name is _____ and I am a _____. I will go first my name is Qwana and I am an Author :>)!!!! Sometimes it still feels like a dream but it is a reality.

Once "You" believe "It" others will too and if you don't believe or aren't fully convinced neither will your audience. BOOOO to you!!!! Now go practice in the mirror ;>)!!!!

Another important benefit is the power of disclosure; once you tell your mother, father, aunty, uncle, cousin, nosey neighbor, classmate, or friend, they won't let you live it down. They will check in, they will ask, they will probe, and most importantly "They" won't let you give up on your dreams and they will keep your accountability in check ;>)!!!! Maybe you shouldn't say anything if, "You ain't bout it, bout it" ;>) (My ode to "Master P" a real go getter) seriously, if you are the real deal strut your stuff and make it happen.

So make sure you go tell it to the mountain; right before you want to lay down your dreams and you begin to feel discouraged the echo will say to you, "How is your Dream coming along?" You had better have an answer or else the nagging will commence LML ;>)!!!! "Howwww Youuuu Doingggg????" (In my best Wendy Williams Voice) ;>)!!!!

236-GPS (God Positioning System)

<u>Friend in My Pocket Prayer</u>

May we all recognize the strength in
Prayer

May we all recognize the strength in
<u>Collective Prayer</u>

May we all recognize when a friend
is in need

May we all recognize that a
friendship can be a brief encounter or
last a lifetime.

May we all recognize the importance
of both.

There is no weakness in needing a
friend there is strength in
recognizing what you are in need of.

Go out and grow and cultivate
friendships then choose one that suits

237-GPS (God Positioning System)

you the best. We have different seasons in our lives where certain friendships are just right or specific to that season. Do not be afraid of seasonal friendship; embrace the diversity of your friend garden ;>)!!!! Friendships can bloom at anytime when you remain open to the process.

Remember friendships are grown and not made ;>)!!!!

Friend In Your Pocket

<u>We Made It, Friend!!!!</u>

Growing along with you is an opportunity of a lifetime and I know I will see you on our next journey ;>)!!!!

Yours truly friend in Heart, Spirit, and especially in your Pocket ;>)!!!! <3

Qwana "BabyGirl" Reynolds Frasier

P.S. Life is Good!!!!

God Bless and Love You Muahhhh <3

Please RP, RT, Screenshot and Share This. (This is for all my Social Networkers)

239-GPS (God Positioning System)

Friend In Your Pocket

Remember your life changed for the better the moment you opened this book.

See You Later ;>)!!!! <3)

240-GPS (God Positioning System)

Luke 6:27

BUT I TELL YOU HEAR ME: love
your enemies, do good to those who
hate you, bless those who curse you,
pray for those who mistreat you.

Luke 6:37-38

DO NOT JUDGE AND YOU WILL
NOT BE JUDGED? Do not
condemn and you will not be
condemned. Forgive, and you will be
forgiven.

Give and it will be given to you. A
good measure, pressed down shaken
together and running over, will be
poured into your lap. For with the
measure you use, it will be measured
to you.

241-GPS (God Positioning System)

Friend In Your Pocket

Remember this life is not like the sneakers or the toy you got for your birthday that you did not like. Remember what you would do at times like this???? You would take those new sneakers and scuff them up, dirty them up etc. As for the unwanted toys they would either mysteriously go missing or get broken up ;>)!!!! I know you remember these days LOL. Messing up the sneakers and toys;(if you were fortunate enough) forced your parents to buy replacements in a hurry.

Just Remember…

This body of life we currently reside in is the only chance and the only

one we will ever have. So… treat it good. If you scuff your life up you will not get another. You will just have to look at the scuffs and learn to appreciate them;>)!!!! If you break your life a part like the toy you did not want you will have to live with the brokenness and allow God to fix/restore you the best way He can.

Appreciate "You" you are important and have a Blessed Divine Purpose!!!!

Because, God Says So;>)!!!!

Friend In Your Pocket

<u>*About the Author*</u>

Good Day My friends, my name is
Qwana "BabyGirl" M. Reynolds-

244-GPS (God Positioning System)

Friend In Your Pocket

Frasier and I am a 36-year-old Black woman from the Bronx, New York. I earned my Bachelors degree of Psychology from City College of New York. I currently reside in Bergen County New Jersey with my Husband, two children, mother, and younger brother. I am the proud mother of two young men 20 (Deshawn "DeDe" (Pronounced "Day Day" Quigley) and 17 (Andre "Moose" Frasier) years old; one is a high school graduate trying to find his way in life and the other will be in the graduating class of 2013, I am a proud mama ;>)!!!! My husband Andre is a New York City Bus Operator and has been for over 13 years; we have been together since I was 14 years old.

245-GPS (God Positioning System)

Friend In Your Pocket

As a growing girl I found solace in school; it was a safe place. I was always engaged in school events like plays, talent shows, peer groups, Kiwanis Builders Club etc. I read ferociously, sometimes reading four and five books a week. Some of my fond memories were having my parents take me to Barnes and Nobles to buy books; those were happy Saturdays. My parents allowed me to build my character and personality at an early age and I thank them for listening at those times. Through it all they always expressed the importance of education.

When I was 11 years old my mother would make a decision that change my whole life for the better. My mother seeing that I was changing and having attitude problems in school would enroll me in a school called the Children's Storefront in Harlem. This school was on the East side of Harlem an area that was plagued by drug abuse and prostitution. I would come to know a marvelous Head Master by the name Ned O'Gorman; he was a famous poet, prose writer, and pioneer of early childhood and education. He was a striking man over six feet tall, who was posed and stern. What I loved about Ned was that he would wait for all the children to come to school as he would sit on the stoop and he would greet you with the biggest hug and tell you how beautiful a child you were. That was

best present every single morning
and this would build my self-esteem.

Hearing how smart, beautiful,
wanted, and welcomed I was a
wonderful lifelong lesson that I
would pass down to my children. I
would flourish in the Storefront
school and I exposed to people,
places, education, experiences,
literature, music, language etc. I
never would have if my mom did not
bring me to this school. The
Children's Storefront was home
mentally, spiritually, and literally; it
was actually set up in historic
brownstones which imprinted the
feeling of home, safety, and peace in
the middle of Harlem in the midst
poverty, neglect and a high crime
rate.

The Children Storefront and Ned
O'Gorman changed my life and
began to strengthen my love for
medicine; I really truly believed I
would become Dr. Reynolds. Then
when I was 14 I had an opportunity
of a lifetime. A man from Vermont
would read about me in the New
York Times, contacted the school
and stated that he would pay for my
education; I wanted to attend Dobb's
Ferry Boarding School for High
School, College and Medical School.
I always wanted to attend Cornell
University and, all I had to do was
write an autobiography. I started to
write but could not stay focused.
Now I understand why... My
childhood trauma was too deep for
me to cope with; it was too fresh at

that time and avoidance was my defense.

Nevertheless I pushed on and attended two public high schools where I successfully earned my high school diploma one year and a half before schedule. During the "Wonder Years" of I met Andre at a Post Valentine's Day Dance at a recreational complex called Milbank in Harlem, the exact date was February 15th 1991, this was my freshman year at Manhattan Center High School for Math and Science also on the East Side of Harlem. I attended Manhattan Center High School for one year; however I would graduate from University Heights High School in the Bronx New York. My relationship with

Friend In Your Pocket

Andre was a "God Sent" due to my home life, which was a mess marred with child molestation, neglect, drug abuse, etc... God knew what I needed and sent help in the form of my then boyfriend now husband Andre Frasier.

During the first year of Andre and I's relationship In June of 1991 I received the gift of my nephew/son with open arms and heart. DeDe (Pronounced Day-Day) was a welcomed addition to the group of children whom I was already responsible for. In my mind one more child would not affect or hinder me. I proudly took on motherhood and assumed responsibility for Deshawn at the tender age of 15. I would attend my new High School

251-GPS (God Positioning System)

with "DeDe" by my side. I was very cautious with who I would leave him with due to my experience of being sexually abused as a child.

From high school I would go on to City College University in Harlem New York where I was now bringing my newborn son Andre better known as, "Moose" with me to every class for the first year of his life and my college life. At City College I took classes that were concentrated on pre medical studies still not giving up the dream to become an obstetrician/gynecologist. I would change my major to Psychology in my upper junior year, so that I could hurry up, graduate, and help support my growing family.

I originally thought that I was medically going to stitch people up and help the healing process; what I know now is that my divine plan was to mentally and spiritually help the healing process; I would help stitch souls and not holes. Yes, God has the final say when you are obedient.

After college I would work as a fashion stylist for emerging hip hop artist and neighborhood fashionistas. In addition I ran my own name belt and clothing company, which was doing really well when I was offered a social work position at a Head Start where my children attended. My mom worked there as the cook, and I had volunteered there for over ten years, it felt like a good transition. This is where I would begin my mission of missionary work. I worked there for two years before leaving to take a Case Manager/Interim Director position with another widely popular non-for profit agency in Harlem.

Totally unfulfilled after working for this agency for three years I left there and embark on a journey into the sub culture of juvenile detention. This would prove to be a defining moment in my life, because juvenile detention shaped my lens and gave me a new focus. After working in juvenile detention for five years I realized that these children were mostly low on hope and self-esteem and if only they had these tools they would thrive. I also realized that they responded well to our talks however when these children went home, to other institutions, back to their communities, and schools; Hope didn't always reside in these places like they did in our program.

Eventually the children would repeatedly come back one by one; the rate of recidivism was astounding. I decided that I wanted to provide a work that would be available to anyone seeking motivation, inspiration, and hope. This experience helped to give rise to, "Friend in Your Pocket"; I am humbled and forever indebted to those children, their families, and my coworkers for allowing me to share some of their most intimate and rawest moments.

255-GPS (God Positioning System)

Friend In Your Pocket

Well there you have it, a synopsis of
my life I tried to condense it but the
words just kept coming. However, in
spite all what you have learned about
my family and I through this brief
bio I want you to understand that I
have prevailed. I do not want people
to walk away with a sense of oh poor
little girl, I want you to take away
from this story that this is also
someone else's story somewhere else
in the world as well. We as a people
have to pay close attention to how
we are connected and affected by
childhood traumas; whether you are
directly impacted or impacted by a
loved one's experience.

I have been blessed over the years to
be exposed to so many different
cultures and as a result I have friends

256-GPS (God Positioning System)

from all walks of life and cultural backgrounds. I have chosen to be an inspiration to anyone that I may come in to contact with and I do so, on an everyday basis through personal and social media outlets. As I talk to people from around the country I realize that we are in the middle of a worldwide cultural awareness movement where people around the world are craving for a blueprint for joy, hope, and deeper human connections. People are weary; single people, married couples, single parents, children, direct care givers, law enforcement, the judicial system, government, local and state agencies etc... Due in part to the widespread violence from domestic abuse, gang culture, lack of education, neglect, lack of strong male and female figures, lack of mental and physical safety etc...

I work with some of the youngest victim's everyday in the juvenile detention system. As a Social Worker I have worked with boys and girls affected by decades of neglect in some of the poorest neighborhoods in the five boros to affluent families from various countries. The resounding and redundant principle that affects the likelihood your child may wind up in my facility is Self-Esteem. I have found that like our children my peers are also succumbing to the premise of peer pressure; the see monkey do monkey do mentality. Though there is no shortage of positive adults and families in entertainment or in our communities we are not intrigued by these examples. We are captivated by drama. I believe that this syndrome can and will be counterattacked with a new life breathed on the importance of family values and a proper upbringing.

I was a product of the Cosby Show and other shows like it that fostered a sense hope to children like me who were going through unspeakable circumstances. These shows would take me from my dismal reality and inspired me to want to go to college, have healthy relationships with my siblings, yearn for better relationships with my parents, and have a high level of respect for my heritage plus so much more. I can

feel a shift in our collective desires
to want the same for our children,
however there is also a collective
feeling of despair and hopelessness.
The time is coming and we the
people who will pave the way and
lead this new grass movement for a
hopeful nation have to rise up, be
counted, and proceed to infiltrate the
voids left behind by these decades of
despair. Our job, my job is to show
the world that our job is a job of joy.
The survivors of the war on drugs,
war on poverty, war on racism, war
on sexism, war on ageism, war on
terror must rise up and show the
world that survivors are teachers and
have a role in the world other than
victim. A victim is only a victim if

they don't teach from their experiences.

Friend in Your Pocket is a series of books that will strive to motivate anyone wanting to enhance and enrich their lives. My goal is to show "My Friends" that they have a story to tell and they should look at their trauma as a gift. However if my reader has not had a personal trauma I strive to make them aware of what their fellow, "Friends" are going through. They should ask themselves the question, how can I help the people around me that have overcome or are in the process of overcoming trauma?

It is my sincere hope that my "Reader Friends" will become more empathetic toward each other hence

261-GPS (God Positioning System)

producing a nation of better humans, teachers, artist, journalists, supervisors, doctors, care givers, judicial personnel, law enforcement agents, CEOs, CFOs etc... Overall becoming people of substance who will begin to make better decisions that will impact our world in a positive matter.

<u>Friend in Your Pocket</u> is a book to be read all at once, once a day, every day, when you are in need etc. This book has no special formatting such as chapters because the thoughts that inspired the book do not have synchronization. When we think it is a random or directly connected to an event as it happens. I want my, "Reader Friends" to be able to connect on a personal level. These thoughts are random like your friend's last post on Facebook, Instagram, or Twitter that caused you to connect through your own experience. This comment form will provoke thought and get a conversation going.

I want my readers to feel as though they are having the best social media connection, in hopes that this will inspire them to want to have more deep thought provoking conversation that can only happen during a one to one conversation with their peers. This book is dinner party talk, cook out/family reunion talk, barber shop talk, hair and nail salon talk, nanny talk, country club talk, gym talk, waiting in line at the airport talk, baby shower talk, birthday party talk, basically I know you are seeing that this conversation is global, ongoing, and never gets old.

Friend in Your Pocket is in tune with the pulse of the people. I set out to have conversations with people that are interested and invested in motivating, inspiring, and spreading hope to others to spark this movement into five alarm blaze. I am interested in our youth and what suggestions they have to save themselves from self-destruction. I want to encourage the youth to see this movement as a partnership that will enable them to see themselves as motivators; this approach will help make them less apt to becoming victims of peer pressure. This Friend In Your Pocket has the potential to spark hope, one youth, one family, and one community at a time with success.

As we can all see we live in a self-professed universe of, "Followers" people following each other over social networks with the hopes that their friends will think that they are cool and will follow them too. Do not get me wrong social networking is a Blessing; however we must understand that this is not how we need to conduct ourselves in real life all the time. It is cool to be in love with yourself, have high standards, and demand more human connections rather than just a like or a comment or re tweet or re post. The world has to re-embrace the human connection. The Human

Friend In Your Pocket

Connection shall prevail and not lose to our beloved Internet connection. The two connections must find a way to cohabitate with each other in our world. I am hopeful that the two can be successfully married for the upward movement of future generations to come.

This small pocketbook with less than 300 pages will have a deep impact. This short sweet, sincere, and to the point work has no fluff, it is powerful and engaging from start to finish. This reader will have our "Friend Base" thirsty for more and for as long as I have breathe in my lungs and energy to type these pages "Friend in Your Pocket" will tackle relevant questions and situations we ponder daily, with vitality, humanity,

quotes, humor, experiments, etc...
This mission will be completed
without rhetoric and page fillers.

There is no book on the market that I
am aware of such as this. As with all
testimony, this experience is unique
like a set of fingerprints. This book is
spiritual, spirit filled, and humorous
throughout, leaving no stone
unturned. The look of this book must
evoke a sense of joy before you open
it. Artist/creators rule the world.
Those that create change the
landscape of our world. With "Friend
in Your Pocket" we will now have a
platform for new artist to emerge and
this journey is their very own "Open
Mic Night" audience where everyone
interested with being enlightened
will appreciate this work of art.

267-GPS (God Positioning System)

Friend In Your Pocket

Sustainable Joy for All is the Mantra of, "Friend In Your Pocket" Your, "Spirit Personal Trainer". Sounds and feels awesome to me, what do you think ;>)????

Thank You and God's Blessing To All Muahhhh <3 ;>)!!!!

Respectfully,

Qwana M. "BabyGirl" Reynolds-Frasier

Your Friend In Your Pocket ;>)!!!!